Lost Restaurants
OF
ASHEVILLE

Lost Restaurants

OF

ASHEVILLE

———————————————————— NAN K. CHASE

AMERICAN PALATE

Published by American Palate
A Division of The History Press
Charleston, SC
www.historypress.com

First published 2019

Manufactured in the United States

ISBN 9781467142311

Library of Congress Control Number: 2019950046

For restaurant workers everywhere

Contents

CONTENTS

Acknowledgements

I am indebted to the staff and board members of the North Carolina Collection at Asheville's Pack Memorial Library for their support and encouragement over months of research. They are the custodians of a great legacy. Above all, the technical expertise and enthusiasm of "amateur history sleuth" Terry Burgin Taylor made it possible to compile and process the vintage photographs in this book. Thank you.

A number of individuals and organizations in Asheville shared lore and photos. In particular, I want to thank photographer Andrea Clark for her gracious permission to use images housed at the North Carolina Collection; in addition, my thanks go to Biltmore Farms, LLC, New Belgium Brewing Company, Explore Asheville Convention & Visitors Bureau, Woolworth Walk, Biltmore Village, historian and architect Robert Griffin, Chantal Saunders of the old Burgermeister's, Asheville historian Rob Neufeld and fifth-generation Asheville native Sherrye Coggiola for their contributions.

Introduction

A sheville has been a popular tourist stop for two centuries, since the first stagecoaches arrived from the hot lowlands in the early 1800s, and good eating has always been part of the attraction. That's because Asheville sits in a land of plenty: fertile soil, moderate temperatures and abundant rainfall have helped the region produce every kind of food and beverage imaginable. An army of talented chefs and cooks has interpreted those raw materials for the last two hundred years. Today, Asheville has a well-deserved worldwide reputation as a dining destination where freshness reigns.

This book concentrates on thirty-two restaurants, cafés and diners that were popular during much of the twentieth century, starting just before 1900 and ending in 2018 but concentrating on the decades between World War I and the 1990s. This fascinating period spans the horse-and-buggy days and the internet age in the space of just a few generations.

Lost Restaurants of Asheville is a social history that reveals how people lived—what they ate, what they wore, where they worked, how they traveled—and how American society changed over the course of those years.

During my research, several themes emerged: the intense work ethic of immigrants who arrived in Asheville almost penniless yet shaped the city's restaurant scene, the close personal relationships that developed between proprietors and their customers and the devastating effects of Jim Crow racial segregation that existed formally in Asheville until the 1960s—and informally long after that.

This narrative follows the arc of time and is organized as closely as possible by the year each restaurant began operation. Only one diner—Tastee Diner in West Asheville—remains continuously open today, and that one is included because the latest change of ownership considerably altered the tone of the place. But more than half the restaurant properties listed in this book still have some kind of food service going on at the same address.

It was not possible to include every restaurant from Asheville's twentieth-century history. There were so many hundreds of establishments during that time. But this selection shows the city's personality.

A note about newspaper resources. The local newspaper, today's *Asheville Citizen-Times*, has had many different names since its inception, including the *Asheville Times*, the *Asheville Citizen* and the *Asheville Citizen and Times*. In most cases, whatever the name at the original reference, I credit *Asheville Citizen-Times*; today's comprehensive *Citizen-Times* database lists all variations simply as the *Asheville Citizen-Times*, and this consistency should make further online research easier.

Enjoy these stories in little bites or in one big feast. I hope you'll be hungry for more.

CHAPTER 1

Gross Restaurant

Bridging Old and New

G ross Restaurant spanned two eras of Asheville's modern history, between the horse-and-buggy days of the late nineteenth century and the jet age after World War II, doing business continuously and in various forms and names for half a century.

Always located in the heart of downtown Asheville, the Gross Restaurant—sometimes a hot dog stand and sandwich shop, sometimes more upscale—represented an enduring feature of the city, as immigrants streamed in from all over the world to make a new, American life in the mainstream culture.

The Grosses were a Jewish family, part of Asheville's large and influential community of Jews who fled persecution abroad and found their Golden Land in the southern Appalachian Mountains. Myers, Swartzberg, Lipinsky, Blomberg, Sternberg, Dave—all helped shape the burgeoning tourist town in businesses ranging from retail clothing to steel manufacture, medicine to cars. For the Grosses, the restaurant trade was the ticket.

During the 1930s, David Gross was known as the "man with the biggest family and the tiniest business in town." One version of his café was no more than a roofed-over outdoor passageway, while one family photo shows his ten children lined up, stair-step fashion, from toddler to preteen. A slightly older image shows seven Gross children, four of them formally dressed and seated in two-wheeled carts pulled by goats, with three more children clustered near their dad.

David Gross was born in Hungary in 1865 and moved to the United States—and possibly Asheville—eight years later. Asheville's tourism trade

The big David Gross family. *North Carolina Collection, Pack Memorial Public Library, Asheville, North Carolina.*

began to boom in 1880, when railways first arrived. Those early boom times would last until 1930, when a local bank crash wiped out most public funds and ushered in fifty years of civic decline; Asheville's twenty-first-century boom as a "foodie" destination would take further decades of struggle to achieve.

The first mention of a "D. Gross Restaurant" in Asheville was an 1896 newspaper account of improvements to an existing establishment: "The storeroom adjoining D. Gross' restaurant on Court Place, with his restaurant stock, is being repapered and the front painted. Electric fans have been placed in the room."

Photographs of the Asheville City Hall building that stood from 1892 until 1926 document a bit of the Gross Restaurant history: in a 1909 picture, "David Gross's Restaurant," identified as a lunch room, is shown next door to that handsome dark-brick civic building. As Pack Square was enlarged and a new city hall built farther to the east, Gross's business had already relocated, probably to 5½ Broadway nearby, in 1917. It was that same year when a Gross Restaurant first appears in an Asheville City Directory, as an "eatinghouse," and about the same time that some of his sons may have been working as cooks, soda jerks and, in one case, a bellboy at the posh new Langren Hotel nearby.

Not only did the Gross Restaurant represent the immigrant dream in Asheville, but it also demonstrated what has always made Asheville a wonderful city for dining: the surrounding countryside has for centuries produced nearly everything that discerning diners and inventive chefs could desire. Farms and hunting lands on every side could supply the city with fresh milk and eggs; tender beef, chicken, turkey, pork and trout; fruit of endless variety; venison and other game; and tasty cornmeal for all sorts of breads and cakes. The only early imports were salt, pepper and coffee, while eventually the railroads made possible speedy delivery of seafood from the Carolina coast.

Even with railroads bringing the outside world to Asheville, local transportation remained primitive (as did public sanitation). It wasn't uncommon, for some years after 1900, to see oxen pulling covered wagons as they lumbered into town from nearby farm communities, loaded with foodstuffs, although the city already had an electric streetcar system and the automobile was coming into use. A twenty-mile trip into town would take a day and a half by ox.

As late as 1919, there was still a demand for livery services in Asheville, as visitors arriving by train were able to rent horses and carriages for excursions into the wild country of waterfalls and deep woods.

This was the busy, jumbled-up backdrop for Gross Restaurant.

The Great Depression hit Asheville hard, and among the many restaurateurs forced to close or downsize, Gross improvised by running a hot dog and ham sandwich operation in a "narrow alleyway between a three-story building and a lunch wagon on Broadway."

The years rolled on, and David Gross turned operations over to two of his sons, Charles and Leon; the name changed to Gross Brothers Restaurant. The location was now back on Pack Square in a long, narrow building that made for extremely compact booth seating at breakfast, lunch and dinner.

Alas, following a remodeling that added a mezzanine to accommodate more diners, some newly installed equipment malfunctioned. The year was 1939, and in the middle of the night, the grease in a deep fryer exploded. Flames spread quickly, and four of Asheville's five fire companies were needed to contain the blaze, as crowds gathered at dawn to watch the drama. Damage amounted to $10,000, a hefty sum, but the Gross brothers vowed to get started with repairs immediately and reopen within two weeks.

In 1945 a newspaper headline proclaimed, "Gross Family Quits Restaurant Business After Half a Century." The brothers sold the restaurant to a Greek immigrant, James Kiritsis, who remodeled again

South Main Street, now Biltmore Avenue, on a busy day before 1910. *North Carolina Collection, Pack Memorial Public Library, Asheville, North Carolina.*

Gross Restaurant had space in this block. *North Carolina Collection, Pack Memorial Public Library, Asheville, North Carolina.*

and ran it for two more years as Gross Restaurant before opening his own place elsewhere downtown.

In those two years, jaunty new print advertisements appeared touting Gross Restaurant as the place for businessmen's lunches, a break for mom or a place for dates. The food now went far beyond steaks and chops: "Roast Long Island Duck with Celery Dressing & Cranberry sauce…Roast Leg of Lamb with mint jelly, natural juices…Roast young Vermont Turkey… Yankee Pot-Roast…Fried Spring Chicken country style…Chicken stew and dumplings…Fried Sugar cured Ham Steak with Hawaiian sauce… Priced from 85¢ up."

CHAPTER 2

Tingle's Cafe

"The Little Cafe with Big Eats"

There really was a Mr. Tingle behind Tingle's Cafe. He was Alvis Malcolm Tingle, a hard worker, an upright guy, a team player, a big Asheville booster when times were down, a friend to many. He was an institution.

Since its founding in 1918, the café that he and his family ran for more than half a century was a memorable stopping place for residents and visitors alike.

Tingle loved the life. There were some famous customers, like Asheville's monumental author Thomas Wolfe and the legendary Walt Disney, who happened to be in town for a while as a professional draftsman. There were the steady local customers, like the businessmen and secretaries dashing in from downtown offices at lunchtime; the late-night crowd craving big sweet slices of pie; the city's mayor; and "the most notorious prostitute in town," according to historian Bob Terrell. "It was a fine and unusual eating place."

And there were the out-of-town visitors—tourists streaming into Asheville who might (just might) need directions to a local attraction or the visiting sportsmen who might (just might) need their newly bagged game or their caught-this-morning mountain trout cleaned, cooked and served up for a modest service charge. Busy shoppers in downtown Asheville might need a place to hold packages for a while…glad to do it.

Not only was Alvis Tingle eager to help out the dining public, but he was also adept at promoting his services and successes.

Owner Alvis M. Tingle at Tingle's Cafe coffee urn. *North Carolina Collection, Pack Memorial Public Library, Asheville, North Carolina.*

Fancy ceiling at Tingle's Cafe. *North Carolina Collection, Pack Memorial Public Library, Asheville, North Carolina.*

By the time of Asheville's big bank crash, in 1930, and during the devastation of the Great Depression that followed, Alvis Tingle had built up considerable goodwill and presumably some capital, so he pitched in to help however he could. The restaurant stayed open all day and all night during the Depression, which meant a lot of extra jobs and some extra cash injected into the economy. Early on, in 1933, Tingle's adopted the National Restaurant Code proposed by President Franklin Roosevelt's National Recovery Act that would support wages levels and working hours, and Tingle took out newspaper ads to underscore the fact. (In 1935, Tingle's was a place where men could apply for logging jobs, and during World War II, Tingle's was a navy recruiting station.)

In the most ambitious Depression-era tourism publicity effort, Tingle's signed on as one of nearly fifty sponsors of the "Welcome to Asheville Motorcade" of 1934. "DO YOUR PART! HELP INVITE the MILLIONS in FLORIDA, GEORGIA AND S.C. to ASHEVILLE *this Season!*" implored a big ad in

Lots of seating options at Tingle's Cafe. *North Carolina Collection, Pack Memorial Public Library, Asheville, North Carolina.*

the *Asheville Citizen-Times*. That ten-day excursion might have been meant to lift the participants' spirits if nothing else, for the itinerary included a chance to stop by "Charleston, Augusta, Savannah and St. Augustine" while meeting with prospective travelers to Asheville, also known as Land of the Sky.

Mostly, though, Mr. Tingle liked to meet and greet right in front of his café, which had first gotten a start as a fruit stand at 29 Broadway and then as a confectionary shop. His obituary in 1951, when he died at age seventy-six, told the story.

> *Tingle saw the need for selling food with soft drinks to tourists, so he placed a small gas stove in the front window with a large pastry display on the sidewalk to be viewed by passerby* [sic].
>
> *While cooking, Tingle could give tourists directions and take care of packages they might not wish to carry with them. It was always his*

Tingle's Cafe offered handy tourist information. *North Carolina Collection, Pack Memorial Public Library, Asheville, North Carolina.*

philosophy to believe in everyone and consider a man honest until found otherwise. Pies, cakes and other foods were in easy reach of the customer. After the customer had eaten, Tingle would ask him what he had consumed, and collect accordingly.

As late as the mid-1940s, the entire back cover of the Tingle's Cafe menu was given over to tourist information, including the ready availability of convenient canned foods and takeout orders.

Ah, the food! Tingle's newspaper ads jumped out of a sea of gray ink with their mouthwatering appeal:

Two nice pieces of chicken. Dumplings
Seasoned well. Hot rolls. Corn
Muffins. Coffee, tea or milk

Bowl of Home-Made Soup and
Nice Fried Trout. Coffee

Country Style Steak you can cut with a fork
Milk Fed fried chicken
Homemade doughnuts, good coffee
Homemade sausage

Select Oysters Fried or Stewed
Barbecue sandwiches
OUR SWISS
CHEESE SANDWICH
Will go good with a Bottle of
BUDWEISER

The selection of homemade pies was a major draw—lemon meringue, chocolate, cherry and more—and if a piece of cherry pie had a pit in it, the diner got a complimentary cigar.

Tingle's outgrew its original location and in 1941 moved into the remodeled building next door, 27 Broadway, for more space. The décor was reliant on fancy tilework and lots of patterns. At that time, the restaurant followed a common practice in racially segregated Asheville: white waitresses served diners, but African American staff worked behind the scenes. Help wanted ads laid it out in stark terms: "colored man or

Menu from Tingle's Cafe. *North Carolina Collection, Pack Memorial Public Library, Asheville, North Carolina.*

woman with pleasant personality to bake rolls, biscuits, etc.…good colored man, good pay, good hours…colored girls to buss dishes, dry silver and do maids' work…colored woman to do salads and silverware."

On an almost mundane level, by comparison, Tingle's was the scene of one of Asheville's most spectacular grease fires one morning in 1953. Flames shot up through vent work, through the second floor and the third floor to the roof. Before the conflagration was brought under control, thousands of people had gathered on the street to watch.

Eventually, the Tingle family opened a second location, Tingle's Too, out to the west on Patton Avenue. And, as often happens with family businesses, by the third generation, interest waned. The original Tingle's closed in 1973 and was followed there by a string of other restaurants and

The white serving staff at Tingle's Cafe. *North Carolina Collection, Pack Memorial Public Library, Asheville, North Carolina.*

The African American staff around a Christmas tree at Tingle's Cafe. *North Carolina Collection, Pack Memorial Public Library, Asheville, North Carolina.*

The big fire at Tingle's Cafe. *North Carolina Collection, Pack Memorial Public Library, Asheville, North Carolina.*

Tingle's Cafe was paved in tile. *North Carolina Collection, Pack Memorial Public Library, Asheville, North Carolina.*

bars in the next few decades, including a second try with the name Tingles and the same retro look. Nowadays, an Italian bistro called Strada Italiano occupies the spot. It's a feel-good location conveniently situated on a busy street, and a whiff of nostalgia still lingers.

CHAPTER 3

Hot Shot Cafe

"Best of the All-Night Beaneries"

When a restaurant stays in business for more than eighty years, it develops a personality all its own. And when it closes, the customers mourn it like an old friend or a member of the family. That was the case with the Hot Shot Cafe, which opened in Biltmore Village in 1925 and closed in 2007. Strictly a local hangout, the Hot Shot was known as the place to go when you needed a hot meal and a cup of coffee or three in the middle of the night, no matter who you were. "The night owl trade," it was called. The café glowed like an oasis "in the desert of the night." The ambiance at 2:00 a.m. was "singular," to put it mildly, and Hot Shot earned the informal title of Asheville's most colorful diner.

"Insomniacs, shift workers, late-night revelers," "doctors, nurses, reporters, policemen, firefighters," everyone "from diplomats to derelicts" loved the Hot Shot. "Socialites in tuxedos and ball gowns joined railroad men and truckers enjoying a "stick-to-the-ribs breakfast."

Even underage drinkers—teenagers then, grandparents today—considered the Hot Shot Cafe a refuge where they could sit, bleary-eyed, until they sobered up enough to drag themselves home to sleep off their youthful hangovers. Asheville has always been a hard-drinking town.

Hot Shot was rough around the edges but not considered really rough. There were fights—a few of them pretty big—but mostly they got taken outside, and there were practical jokes that got out of hand. In the bad old

Hot Shot Cafe, an all-night diner in Biltmore Village. *Courtesy of Robert Griffin.*

days of the 1970s, when crime in Asheville escalated, the café once got hit for nearly $800 in merchandise and cigarettes.

Over the years, stars of stage and screen dropped by the Hot Shot—often in the wee hours of the night, after performances—and left indelible impressions. Country musician Travis Tritt drove there in his pea-green Cadillac, and further back, according to newspaper columnist Bob Terrell, the actor Lee Marvin, while filming a movie in Asheville, showed up drunk and instructed the waitress to pour everyone a drink, on him. She promptly brought out a coffee pot to make the rounds! Members of the band Smashing Pumpkins ate there twice.

Homemade biscuits and gravy formed the backbone of the Hot Shot's hearty round-the-clock menu, perfect for absorbing any excess. Pork chops, steaks, soups, omelets, vegetable plates, sandwiches, daily specials and tempting desserts—standard country fare with a twist. Some of the staff could remember fifteen orders at a time without jotting them down.

The whole crazy scene (a portrait of Jesus keeping watch by the door) appeared through a fog bank of cigarette smoke. "When you walked in, you peered through clouds of smoke haze to see who was sitting in the back," wrote Bob Terrell affectionately. He and his fellow reporters on the night shift would go as a group to the Hot Shot after work.

"Nobody paid any attention to the smoke then. Everybody smoked,… Those with the best nostrils could sit in one booth and tell what folks in the adjoining booth were smoking—Camels, Luckies, Raleighs (whew!), Philip Morris. If you were out of cigarettes, all you had to do was breath[e] and you'd smoke like all the rest."

For the first fifty years at least, there was no key to the front door, for the simple reason that Hot Shot Cafe never closed.

Hot Shot got its start around 1925 as a small hot dog and soda stand "no bigger than a piano box" at the corner of Biltmore Avenue and Lodge Street, in Biltmore Village. That's where streetcars from downtown Asheville turned around, and the location worked so well that the stand stayed open twenty-four hours a day from the beginning. The founders were Jim and Minny (or Minnie) Jennings, who, according to family legend, left the coal fields of Kentucky pushing a wheelbarrow that held all their belongings. An alternative narrative told how the Jenningses were stranded in Asheville when a train they were riding derailed. Anyway, they stayed.

Twenty-five years on, the café had grown larger, and then it moved just a few doors down on Lodge Street when a gas station took over the corner lot. In 1971, Charles Jackson bought the business, although Mrs. Jennings stayed on the staff for a while.

Jackson's biggest challenge as a businessman may have been during the energy crisis of the mid-1970s, when state regulations mandated restrictive indoor temperature limits. Limiting nighttime temperatures was tough on a twenty-four-hour business, and in order to stay open nights for his faithful third-shift customers, he had to set the thermostat down to fifty-five degrees Fahrenheit. Ten years earlier he had started closing on Mondays, but now he closed on Sunday nights as well, and he had to use residual heat from grills and ovens to supplement the heater.

As fast-food franchises took hold in Asheville, offering all-night service and drive-through breakfasts, it became harder for Hot Shot to compete. With new owners, new hours followed. The Hot Shot lost a bit of steam.

The Garson brothers bought the place and invested $375,000 in repairs after major flooding in 2004 swept away everything but a can opener, but then they went retail.

You can look today at 18 Lodge Street but see no trace of the original Hot Shot.

Hot Shot Cafe, in business more than eighty years. *Courtesy of Robert Griffin.*

FEEDING A CROWD

The *Asheville Citizen-Times* in 1997 shared this restaurant-scaled recipe from Hot Shot Cafe cook Josephine Wilson:

Southern Country Style Steak

Use 40 pieces of cubed steak. Dip steak in batter of 2½ pounds of flour, 1 tablespoon of salt, 1 tablespoon of pepper, 1 can of evaporated milk and one can of water.

Fry steak in hot cooking oil until golden brown, then reduce heat and cook steak until done. For the steak gravy, leave two cups of the cooking oil and mix in 3½ cups of flour, stirring at all times until medium brown. Add ½ gallon of warm water, one can of evaporated milk and cook until gravy thickens. Pour gravy over steak and cook for ½ hour. The steak will be tender enough to cut with a fork and very tasty.

CHAPTER 4

S&W Cafeteria

An Art Deco Dining Destination

How could something work so well for so long…and then go completely off the rails? That's the essential question about downtown Asheville's most outrageous—most decorative and once most popular—commercial building: the 1929 architectural masterpiece built as the S&W Cafeteria, Asheville's "crown jewel" and its "highest pinnacle of Art Deco," according to newspaper coverage.

Only in Asheville and only at the apex of its 1920s expansionist glory could a building like the S&W Cafeteria become a reality. The building still stands today at 56 Patton Avenue in the midst of a new tourist boom, and not much has changed except for one crucial difference: for more than fifty years through the middle of the twentieth century the S&W was a community gathering place in the city center where thousands of people would eat on a typical day. Friends met there, families dined together and grew up there. Once that function was lost, on the day in 1974 when the restaurant moved to something called a mall, the good times were over.

Since then, the S&W Cafeteria building has beckoned to numberless entrepreneurs from the southeast corner of Pritchard Park. But every subsequent tenant at that location—and there have been dozens—has gone belly up, some of them quite fast. Still, hope springs eternal.

The building itself is to blame, for its creator, the architect Douglas D. Ellington, visualized it as one decorative, functional whole. Terrazzo floors

A parade float in front of S&W Cafeteria. *North Carolina Collection, Pack Memorial Public Library, Asheville, North Carolina.*

and molded plaster ceilings, travertine marble and brass scrollwork and porcelain tiles. Bold colors, gilded bits, arches and zigzags, on and on.

The architect himself, who also designed the Asheville City Building and Asheville High School, described his approach:

> *The new S. and W. [sic] Cafeteria building is a result of applying unhampered architecture to an individual commercial need: or more nearly, the evolving of an original specific architecture for a specific business structure in a specific site within a specific community....*
>
> *Each proportion is related to all other proportions, each surface is related to all other surfaces, each bit of color is related to all other color motives, and in turn all of these are related to each other.*

In practice, that meant that once the original occupant left, no one else could make alterations without affecting the look, the operation and the feel of that edifice (and now the building is locked in place in the National Register

Pritchard Park with S&W Cafeteria in the background. *North Carolina Collection, Pack Memorial Public Library, Asheville, North Carolina.*

of Historic Places). No one could replicate the atmosphere of excitement, and once the major retailers left downtown Asheville for various new malls in the 1970s, the whole commercial district was a ghost town for years.

"In the days when eating out was a luxury, going to the S&W was a special occasion," wrote one nostalgic observer.

Said another, "Every foray into the city mandated Sunday best. At the S&W, by the time you emerged out of the chute that encased the dining room, it was a coming-out akin to what a debutante must feel, knowing you were on parade with a tray of food that must be balanced gracefully, in the cleanest clothes you owned."

Quite simply: "My family used to go to the S&W when it was the greatest cafeteria on the planet."

For white people, that is. S&W Cafeterias opened to black patrons only in the 1960s.

The cafeteria operation was the brainchild of two World War I buddies, Frank O. Sherrill and Fred R. Webber, who together managed the tearoom at a Charlotte, North Carolina department store. In 1920, the two men struck out on their own, and their cafeteria chain grew to include outlets throughout the South.

The goal was to serve home-style cooking at low prices. One of the most expensive items was tenderloin steak, at twenty-five cents, while other selections cost five or ten cents. The menu changed daily, and to keep waste to a minimum, the staff weighed the previous day's sales, the weather forecast and other factors.

Sherrill and Webber opened their first Asheville cafeteria in 1922, remodeling what had been an opera house on Patton Avenue. "Business was very, very good from the beginning," Sherrill said in an interview, and by 1929, architect Douglas Ellington had completed his commission for their new building across the street.

The interior was as richly decorated as the exterior. There was a large main room with space for three buffet lines. There was a mezzanine and side rooms, private rooms upstairs, a basement and an elaborate double stairway;

Buffet serving line at downtown S&W Cafeteria. *North Carolina Collection, Pack Memorial Public Library, Asheville, North Carolina.*

it was a collection of spaces, a "warren." Local legend has it, according to Asheville writer Carole Currie in an *Asheville-Citizen Times* column, that there was a third-floor "lawyer's table" where local attorneys could hole up at lunchtime in "a drab little room" and talk among themselves during lunch to discuss cases informally: "A valuable by-product was the salve and lubrication that those lunches provide for colleagues in a profession that is naturally adversarial." These colleagues considered themselves "S&W brothers" who would do each other no wrong in the courtroom.

In the 1940s, the S&W typically served 3,500 meals a day—breakfast, lunch and dinner—and up to 5,000 in the busy tourist season. Every civic group in town seemed to hold meetings there, from the United Textile Workers of America to the Buncombe County Republican Club to the Latin Club of Lee H. Edwards High School. Thursday nights were "maid's night out" in Asheville, and so Thursday night became Family Night at the S&W, with movies and games for children and specially priced kiddie plates.

The grand stairway at S&W Cafeteria downtown. *North Carolina Collection, Pack Memorial Public Library, Asheville, North Carolina.*

The soaring S&W Cafeteria dining room. *North Carolina Collection, Pack Memorial Public Library, Asheville, North Carolina.*

Trouble started in 1973 as management announced that a second Asheville S&W would soon open at the new Asheville Mall, with the original cafeteria remaining. But by 1974, the S&W on Patton Avenue was shuttered. Soon a Dale's Cafeteria took its place, but it went bust within months, and then the building stayed empty for ten years, decaying.

The mezzanine level at S&W Cafeteria. *North Carolina Collection, Pack Memorial Public Library, Asheville, North Carolina.*

S&W Cafeteria at an unsuccessful mall location. *North Carolina Collection, Pack Memorial Public Library, Asheville, North Carolina.*

Eventually, as downtown Asheville's fortunes rose, developers took a fresh look at the S&W Cafeteria. One after another, they professed to "love" the building and wanted to restore it to vibrancy. A comedy club, a Greek diner, condominiums, a seafood pub, a wine bar, a coffeehouse, a bakery, more restaurants, a music club—they all tanked. "I'm never going to sell this building," declared one developer shortly before filing for bankruptcy. In recent years, even Douglas Ellington's great-nephews tried and failed.

The latest contenders, as of late 2019, will be a high-powered combine of local Highland Brewery and star restaurateur Meherwan Irani; a new taproom and four different food purveyors will try to fill the space profitably and with hints of Roaring Twenties style. Time will tell.

The ultimate irony was that the S&W Cafeteria that moved to Asheville Mall in 1974 closed for good in 1981. Its design, featuring fast-moving buffet "wheels" that could serve huge crowds without lines, wasn't popular with diners.

CHAPTER 5

F.W. Woolworth Co.

Soda Fountain with a Side of History

Consider the ice cream sundae: sweet and cold, melt-in-the-mouth smooth and with chewy nuts to make it even better.

Or the hot dog: still sizzling, with dribbles of mustard and ketchup, dollops of minced onion and slaw, all stuffed into a fat, fresh bun.

Simple pleasures.

Sometimes the simple pleasures hold greater import. Such is the case with the F.W. Woolworth Co. lunch counter and soda fountain, which opened on stylish Haywood Street in July 1939. Before that store closed for good, in 1993, the lunch counter had been the site of a landmark event in the civil rights era and Asheville's history: the city's earliest desegregation of its once all-white restaurants and cafés, in 1960.

Fortunately for history lovers, the Woolworth lunch counter and soda fountain live on after years when they were abandoned to the ravages of time and free enterprise. It's possible for anyone now to walk right in, take a swivel seat and enjoy a scrumptious treat within those same four walls. The café's current owners, at what today is called the Soda Fountain at Woolworth Walk, respectfully honor that history.

The F.W. Woolworth Co. building on Haywood Street, "one of the most modern in the South," was the second store the company built in Asheville. The first, dating from 1914, was located nearby on Patton Avenue, but when Asheville's *Citizen-Times* newspaper left its 25 Haywood Street address for larger quarters on O. Henry Avenue, Woolworth tore down the remains and built a new three-story, cream-colored structure. At

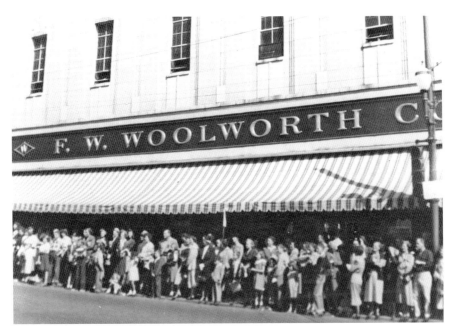

A crowd in front of F.W. Woolworth Co. *North Carolina Collection, Pack Memorial Public Library, Asheville, North Carolina.*

that time, the Woolworth chain was still growing; at one point, it had three thousand stores nationwide.

Oh, that Haywood Street store was pretty! The front was an expanse of "terra cotta and plate glass, set in aluminum frames." Three wide doorways were united under a striped awning, and the name "F.W. Woolworth and Co." sparkled in gold letters on a red background.

The main floor was cavernous, 75 feet wide and 140 feet deep. Decorative finishes included "ornamental plaster mirrors and wood…a combination of South American bella roja and black walnut," and there were twenty-seven sales counters on the main floor, plus a lunch counter and soda fountain.

A "steel and aluminum" grand double stairway descended to the basement; the air-conditioned kitchen that supplied the upstairs dining room was located at the back of the basement. In those days before antibiotics became widespread, kitchen sanitation was of utmost importance, so this kitchen had "buff glaze tile" on the walls and "red quarry tile" on the floors for ease of cleaning. The all-electric kitchen featured a "proof box" for rising yeast doughs and a twin dumbwaiter to take prepared food upstairs.

Sandwiches and sundaes—those were the main draws. The sandwiches were—and are again today—immense, many of them three-deckers: bacon and tomato, baked ham and cheese and top-of-the line chicken salad, originally priced at sixty-five cents. The "Super Deluxe" baked ham sandwich, "sliced very thin and stacked high" on bread roll or toast, cost forty cents. "You Will Like It!" promised the menu.

Even more space on the menu was devoted to fountain treats, like super-jumbo banana splits for thirty-nine cents, malted milkshakes, "squeezed to order" orange juice, ice cream sodas and the delightful-sounding tulip sundaes (ice cream and fresh fruit in season, topped with a choice of syrups plus whipped cream, nuts and cherry for twenty-five cents). And there was home-style apple pie or layer cake for fifteen cents "per cut." For a while, at least, children could pop a balloon holding a piece of paper to see if they had won a banana split for a penny.

In mid-twentieth-century Asheville, Haywood Street was usually jammed with shoppers; the bus lines converged at nearby Pritchard Park, and Woolworth's was a popular place to meet friends and refresh. But African American patrons were not allowed to eat there, although they could cook and serve food.

While other southern cities experienced sometimes violent sit-ins to desegregate lunch counters, Asheville's situation was lower key. It was local high school students, not college students as elsewhere, who took on the responsibility of staging peaceful protests on site. Four Asheville lunch counters, including Woolworth, were thus integrated beginning in August 1960, with negotiations taking half a year before a final agreement was reached.

One of the African American waitresses who had been working at Woolworth during that period, Geneva Tisdale, was given the honor, with two coworkers, of being the first seated under the new rules. She continued to work behind the counter for three more decades.

In 1965, the Woolworth store underwent a quarter-million-dollar top-to-bottom renovation. The lunch counter was expanded to an astonishing 180 feet in length, with room for eighty diners at once. Booths were added with "nomad blue" leather seats topped with light posts á la the Gay Nineties. The grand stairway was modernized with "solid bronze handrails," and a new pet department even sold alligators.

But by the early 1970s, the modernization made no difference. Shopping malls had come to town, and Woolworth announced it would open a second store in one of them. By 1993, the Haywood Street store was no more; for a while, the space was occupied by a Family Dollar discount store. In 1997, the whole Woolworth chain shut down, and in 1999, the Family Dollar, too, closed as downtown Asheville languished.

Enter Scott Sirkin, a property developer new to Asheville who believed the center city had a glorious future before it. He and his wife bought the property and, after rejecting the idea of a single tenant for the storefront, decided to repurpose it as Woolworth Walk, a collection of gallery display nooks for nearly two hundred local craft artists. The project has garnered two prestigious Griffin Awards for Historic Accuracy.

Woolworth Walk has been a great success. The Sirkins brought back the soda fountain in its authentic style. The lunch menu once again features enormous sandwiches and old-fashioned ice cream sodas, sundaes and egg creams. On hot days, it's a cool place to stop for a history lesson and some refreshment.

CHAPTER 6

Silver Dollar Cafe

Island in the Sea of Time

Seventy-seven years. That's a lot of biscuits and gravy.

The Silver Dollar Cafe was a regular place for regular people. Its low-priced menu was unpretentious, just heavy on eggs, grits, biscuits and gravy, fried chicken and meat-and-two-veg. No extra charge for love, comfort and shelter.

The folks who ran the Silver Dollar—and there were only two sets of owners from its beginning in 1934 to the end in 2011—were typical mid-twentieth-century Americans, men and women of humble origins looking to support their families and contribute to their community. They resembled the folks they served: working class and often new to the area. They were colorful, almost like characters on a stage set.

Newspaper reporter Carol Motsinger, in a tribute to the café when it closed, described the customers at Silver Dollar Cafe this way: "These 'ordinary people' are Asheville's taxi drivers. Construction workers and plumbers. Retirees. Nostalgic businessman and the hungover hipsters."

For aging Catherine Dotsikas, one of the later owners and a constant presence, the customers were like family. Motsinger wrote, "No matter their vocation, age or social class, they are always 'honey' or 'baby.'"

If you look closely today at 175 Clingman Avenue, now kind of a shabby-chic biergarten hugging the edge of Asheville's vibrant River Arts District, you may see the ghost of Silver Dollar past. Most recently, the building has been home to the wildly successful All Souls Pizza, but its modest brick silhouette holds a lot of different memories for older native Ashevilleans.

Where All Souls Pizza has given the restaurant's interior an open, casual look, the Silver Dollar was famous for being old-fashioned and unchanging. One observer called the Silver Dollar an "unburied time capsule."

For restaurant reviewer Tracy Mixson, the unvarying past was the charm. "The menus are well-worn, the walls are decorated with faded photos of cowboys and the décor is plastic. But the food is dependable, filling and ample, and the prices are rock-bottom." One critic called it "greasy grub."

When W.J. "Bill" Carter started the Silver Dollar Cafe in 1934, it was first located on Roberts Street, around the corner from the Clingman Avenue location. Here was Asheville's early industrial zone along the banks of the French Broad River, with busy rail yards, a tannery, a cotton mill, stockyards, tobacco warehouses, a racetrack for stock cars and all the hurly-burly that went with those tough livelihoods.

One time, in 1954, at 4:00 a.m., thirty-five-year-old Charles Bishop had one hand "mangled" when he hopped off the freight train he was riding, stumbled and was partially run over. Bishop lay unconscious "for some time" but, once revived, managed to walk to the Silver Dollar Cafe, "where police were notified." He was taken to the closest hospital and then transferred to the Veterans Hospital in Oteen, at Asheville's eastern boundary, where his condition was listed as good.

Bill Carter, the Silver Dollar owner in those days, had come to Asheville from Kansas in 1925, working several different jobs before settling down as the owner of the diner. He sponsored a softball team, and the café served as the meeting place for bowling league referees. And Carter was an avid fisherman, with one twenty-two-inch catch that made the newspaper.

In 1967, after thirty-three years at the Silver Dollar, Carter was ready to retire, and he sold the café to a recent Greek immigrant, Angelo Dotsikas, and his wife, Catherine. Dotsikas was one of a long chain of immigrants who came to Asheville as funds allowed and then helped the next countryman to come over too. Many of these Greek immigrants became restaurant owners, quickly enriching the city's cuisine with well-seasoned dishes and gracious service.

In the early 1970s, the whole Silver Dollar Cafe building was loaded onto a truck bed and moved to Clingman Avenue to make way for construction of a new bridge linking Asheville proper—specifically the kudzu-choked swath where industry was deserting the riverside—with West Asheville. Today, the River Arts District is a bustling collection of hundreds of art studios and a score of highly regarded restaurants and snack shacks, a favorite destination for visitors worldwide. Back then it was just dead.

Silver Dollar Cafe on moving day. *North Carolina Collection, Pack Memorial Public Library, Asheville, North Carolina.*

But almost alone, the Silver Dollar endured, thanks to its regular clientele and its laid-back, anything goes atmosphere. "If you stay in one place for 45 years," Angelo Dotsikas once said, "then you've been a success."

There were a few glimmers of fame and infamy along the way. Sometime movie stars stopped by if they were filming in the area. And sometimes there was crime; in 1973, a break-in yielded $500 in cash, and another time, two men armed with bolt cutters and sledgehammers tried to break in.

Angelo and Catherine Dotsikas kept the place running fifteen hours a day, seven days a week, opening at 6:00 a.m. So after forty-four years operating the café, and by then in their seventies, the couple decided they, too, must retire. "I'm just so tired, honey," Mrs. Dotsikas said. They closed the Silver Dollar Cafe on September 1, 2011, and then went home to "sit down."

By then the River Arts District was hot stuff, growing fast. Trendy restaurants would be a foundation of that growth. The Dotsikases leased the building to a couple from Brooklyn, New York, who promptly opened The Asheville Public (TAP), which harnessed a "fresh, on-trend culinary vision" showcasing "house-made sausages," "South African dried chipped beef" and "salmon cured in green tea." The building had been completely renovated and decorated in a "hip retro style."

That enterprise lasted just over a year before the creative partnership dissolved. Then All Souls Pizza took over. Thanks to a beautifully crafted brick oven and a chef dedicated to using the freshest heirloom flours, the business took off. The *New York Times* gave a favorable review, but the place already had a steady following.

Besides its pizza-licious menu, All Souls has the advantage of a big parking lot—a rarity in central Asheville—and the rambling garden that grows shady and cool on summer evenings.

Chapter 7

Biltmore Plaza Recreation Center

"Dining, Dancing, Fountain, and Bowling"

Asheville's premier tourist attraction is undoubtedly Biltmore Estate, with its eight thousand acres of well-groomed land and its signature 250-room mansion. More than one million visitors stream through the entrance gates every year, which means that almost as many people also get a glimpse of Biltmore Village, the charming collection of buildings just outside the estate.

Biltmore Village has a fascinating history, and the Biltmore Plaza Recreation Center (sometimes written as Biltmore-Plaza) contributed a fair share to the narrative. Just knowing some of the backstory can enhance a visit.

When the Biltmore Plaza opened on July 4, 1942, it featured every kind of World War II–era convenience; even the garbage was refrigerated to keep odors and insects at bay. Nowadays the property, which takes up a whole block between the old railway depot and the beautiful Cathedral of All Souls, is home to a Mexican restaurant called The Cantina at Historic Biltmore Village, a ladies' clothing shop and some vacation rental units upstairs.

Before European explorers and then American settlers reached today's Biltmore Village, that low-lying area was part of the vast Cherokee territory. Situated on the banks of the oft-flooding Swannanoa River, the land later became known as Swannanoa Settlement—a simple farming community—and, after the railroad reached town in 1880, as Asheville Junction, then as Best, then as South Biltmore. Not until 1929 did Biltmore Village get annexed by the City of Asheville.

Dining-Fountain Building and Bowling Club House
"THE BILTMORE-PLAZA" RECREATION CENTER, ASHEVILLE, N. C.

Biltmore Plaza Recreation Center offered a modern look. *North Carolina Collection, Pack Memorial Public Library, Asheville, North Carolina.*

When George Vanderbilt began purchasing innumerable tracts to make up his estate in 1888, he simply bought all of the village properties, including a thriving brick yard, and got rid of the existing homes, businesses, church—and inhabitants. Then he had the swampy ground filled in with 490,000 cubic feet of soil.

A man of artistic sensibilities and orderly ways, Vanderbilt instructed his designers to create a new "manorial village" that would serve as a pleasing entryway to his estate as well as a source of rental income. The aesthetic and functional anchors of the fan-shaped village would be a railroad station, an Episcopal church and estate offices. During nearly two decades of construction, he added a post office and numerous retail shops along the wide paved streets and rows of sturdy cottages to house estate managers, employees and others. The village had its own school, hospital, post office and grocery store, plus ornate street lighting and brick sidewalks. Laundry, butcher shop, drugstore, barbershop, dry goods store, tearoom, livery stables—everything was there.

George Vanderbilt's wife, Edith, was instrumental in creating a commercial weaving industry in Biltmore Village from what remained of a traditional home-based craft. She underwrote the founding of what became Biltmore Estate Industries, makers of fine homespun woolen cloth. The first workshop location, with forty looms, would later become the Biltmore Plaza Recreation Center.

First, though, a devastating flood intervened.

In the summer of 1916, prolonged rains throughout the region produced deadly flooding in Asheville. The Swannanoa River jumped its banks in the pre-dawn hours of July 16, filling streets with water to a depth of fifteen feet. Families fled for their lives, and many properties were severely damaged or destroyed.

Fast-forward a generation. George Vanderbilt had died in 1914, and his wife sold the entire village to one buyer who then was able to resell parcels. The architectural uniformity was broken apart and individual enterprises developed willy-nilly. Mrs. Vanderbilt's weaving shop changed ownership and moved, and the half-timbered mock-Tudor building was lost.

After the Great Depression, the war years brought a boom of prosperity, and the Biltmore Plaza Recreation Center was born. An entire commercial block was dedicated to a Southern Colonial–style brick complex that was billed as "the Crossroads of Western North Carolina."

The concept was straightforward: fun, stylish fun. Pre-television fun. The low-slung building featured indoor and outdoor dining—the patio had "awnings and umbrellas and a barbecue pit"—as well as curb service, twelve "modernly equipped" bowling alleys, "locker and clubhouse facilities" and a soda fountain. Bowling was thirty cents a game; half the maple-clad lanes were duck pin, the rest ten pin, and there were automatic pin setters and "telescorers." The clubhouse facilities were upstairs. The men's locker room had showers, while the ladies' lounge had a "carpeted powder room…with full length mirrors and a desk."

The interior décor was elaborate. "The floors are black terrazzo," read the newspaper coverage of the opening, "and the entire building, including the bowling alleys, is air conditioned." The main-floor dining room held the soda fountain, with seating for thirty-six patrons and further seating in semicircular "Hollywood settees." In addition to mirrored walls, this level would have a two-hundred-foot-long "fresco mural" scrolling around the room, painted in "brilliant colors" by the artist Felix Welks de Weldon. Five phonographic speakers carried mood music throughout the building. "Different types of music will be played at different hours during the day, and the speakers are arranged so as to pick up any radio program of interest," the local newspaper reported. Upstairs, an intimate "candlelight room" had walls papered black and floors carpeted red. A candle burned at each table.

Murals adorned the walls at Biltmore Plaza Recreation Center. *North Carolina Collection, Pack Memorial Public Library, Asheville, North Carolina.*

Elegant dining room at Biltmore Plaza Recreation Center. *North Carolina Collection, Pack Memorial Public Library, Asheville, North Carolina.*

Bowling pins immortalized in terrazzo at Biltmore Plaza Recreation Center. *Photo by Nan K. Chase.*

The menu was far ranging, from sandwiches to café entrées (hours were 10:00 a.m. to midnight). A 1948 sample menu included cream of spinach soup or jellied consommé; a fruit cup or chilled tomato juice; and then flounder, prime rib *au jus*, roast Long Island duckling, Virginia ham with raisin sauce, roast young turkey with cornbread dressing and fresh shrimp and celery salad—nothing priced above $1.50. Vegetable choices were corn on the cob, snowflake potatoes and peas with carrots. For dessert: fresh strawberry shortcake, apple crumb pie and peach cobbler.

Despite all these attractions, the recreation center only operated through the 1950s. It was sold in 1963 and then had a personality change. Eventually, a series of new restaurants occupied part of the space, with offices, retail and residential taking over the rest.

Portions of decorative mosaics—of a bowling ball and pins—remain embedded in the masonry around the building.

CHAPTER 8

The Ritz Restaurant

A Soulful, Doleful Story

So complete was Asheville's racial segregation for nearly a century—following Reconstruction after the Civil War until court-ordered desegregation in the early 1960s—that black citizens supported their own multifaceted business district downtown. The geographic limits, known as The Block, were roughly defined by Biltmore Avenue, Eagle Street, Valley Street and Hilliard Avenue. In fact, not until 1963 did Asheville's city council repeal an ordinance banning African Americans from buying property in predominantly white neighborhoods.

For more than fifty of those years, The Ritz Restaurant, or simply The Ritz, was an institution on The Block, as legendary founder Erline McQueen served up breakfasts of salmon croquettes and dinners of mouthwatering fried chicken and tender beef stew. She arose at 2:00 or 3:00 a.m. to start cooking and stopped serving at 10:00 or 11:00 p.m. On Sundays, the restaurant opened at noon for the after-church crowd.

In the best of times, The Block bustled with customers coming and going from black-owned shops and professional offices: doctors and dentists, barbers and hairdressers, photographers and music teachers, real estate and insurance agents, attorneys, druggists, undertakers, plus sweet shops, restaurants, florists, tailoring shops and jewelers. And there were fraternal organizations like the Black Masons, the Waiters and Bellmen's Club and the Negro Democratic Club, as well as churches, a branch library and a kindergarten. There was a YMCA facility in the massive Young Men's Institute that George Vanderbilt constructed for the black craftsmen who helped create his mansion; the YMI Building still stands.

"It was a safe area," recalled Julia Ray, owner of a cleaner's establishment on The Block and widow of a funeral director. "Everybody knew everybody, and nobody was unkind."

But the good times didn't last forever. First came dislocations caused by the drugs and crime that seeped in after World War II. Then legally mandated desegregation provided the final, painful irony: once African American shoppers could patronize white businesses, the heart of the black business community on The Block stopped beating. Words like "faded," "rough," "blighted," "dusty" and "wrecked" described the desolate scene. Urban renewal projects in the 1970s gutted the close-knit black residential community nearby, almost guaranteeing that The Block could never be replicated as it once was.

From 1946, when Mrs. McQueen and her husband, Hooney, a Pullman railway porter, opened The Ritz, until 2000, when she retired and the restaurant closed, the place was a beacon for local folks and for the African American stars of sports and music who traveled through Asheville, big names like Louis Armstrong and Duke Ellington. Local lore has the renowned performer Paul Robeson singing with a local church choir when he came to visit brothers of his who married local women.

Asheville Blues team of the Negro Southern League around 1946. *North Carolina Collection, Pack Memorial Public Library, Asheville, North Carolina.*

The Ritz Restaurant had meeting rooms upstairs. *Photo by David Black, North Carolina Collection, Pack Memorial Public Library, Asheville, North Carolina.*

At first, The Ritz was located at the corner of Eagle and South Market Streets in the three-story 1930 Del Cardo Building with its fine brickwork and unusual angled façade. Five years later, the McQueens moved the restaurant around the corner, just next door, to what had been the Black Masonic Temple, at 42–44 South Market. There it stayed.

While The Ritz occupied the ground floor of that structure, the two upper floors at first held rooms for the American Federation of Musicians and the Elks Club. In 1956, the McQueens paid $13,000 for the whole building and turned the upstairs into a boardinghouse. Among the residents was future baseball Hall of Fame slugger Willie Stargell, who for a while played for the Asheville Tourists team. Scores of musicians also called the place home; jazz was huge, and band members needed someplace to stay. The whole building came to be called The Ritz Building.

Not only was The Ritz known for its food, homemade from fresh local ingredients, but Erline McQueen's warm welcome was also famous. She was a dynamo and later in life was an activist in Asheville civic affairs and downtown rehabilitation efforts.

She once described her culinary approach to a reporter at the *Asheville Citizen-Times*:

> *In the morning we had grits, homemade biscuits, sausage, salmon croquettes, scrambled eggs, juices and jelly. I think I'm the person who started sausage biscuits and ham biscuits. The working men would come by and didn't have time to eat. And I gave them two sausage biscuits and a cup of coffee for 30 cents.*
>
> *The menu for lunch was fresh stew beef, chicken, country ham and pork chops and veal chops. And we had sweet potato pie and apple pie and homemade cakes.*

Despite modest fare like beans and rice or fried fish, contemporary accounts called The Ritz "elegant" and "a showplace."

As Erline McQueen grew older, her role at The Ritz changed. In 1994, she sold the building to a local man but continued to help with cooking and operations. In 2000, she hung up her apron for good and retired. The restaurant closed, and as often happens when an original owner passes from the scene, nothing stuck.

From 2001 to 2003, after a $300,000 makeover, there was Mr. Gene's Family Restaurant, but that business moved away and another set of owners appeared. They created a new Ritz. "It makes me feel really, really good,"

Erline McQueen proclaimed. This time, the owners promised not to change the name while Mrs. McQueen was alive. She was an honored guest at the opening and greeted diners as in olden times; her image was part of the marketing logo, and she gave her blessing to menu items.

Erline McQueen, a farmer's daughter from the mountains, died in 2007 at age ninety-five. At that point, The Ritz became One Love Two Jamaican Restaurant. A succession of other restaurants and clubs went in and out of The Ritz Building.

Asheville's "ever-evolving local dining scene" melded with its ever-evolving local real estate scene. Efforts to revive The Block dragged on for years, but as property values suddenly soared, the mix became more upscale. The remains of the Ritz Building are now incorporated into the eight-story residential project behind it, looking like a small brick medallion embedded in a tall glass slab.

CHAPTER 9

Paradise Restaurant

Asheville Gets a Taste of the Orient

Modern twenty-first-century Asheville has every type of ethnic restaurant under the sun: Indian, Ethiopian, Korean, Salvadoran, Nepalese, Greek, Thai and more than a few fun fusions. But when the Paradise Restaurant opened, just after New Year's Day 1947, the place was exotic, a taste of the Orient, as Asia was called back then. This Chinese American restaurant, located at 19 Broadway in a busy commercial district of downtown Asheville, quickly became a family favorite in the city.

Throughout the late 1940s, '50s, '60s, '70s, '80s and most of the following decade, the Paradise Restaurant endured, not closing until 1997. For fifty years, until just before Asheville's current restaurant frenzy took off, Paradise Restaurant was a place where generations of local diners could dip into a foreign cuisine without leaving home.

Specialties included platters of chow mein and egg foo young, won ton soup and bowls billowing with white rice (the rice washed four or five times before cooking to remove starch and attain the desired fluffy texture). Some of the allure came from rarity value; many of the ingredients weren't available in Asheville at the time, but Paradise Restaurant had its own supplier in the Wing Lee Yuen Chinese farms of Florida.

Billed as "Asheville's Only Chinese & American Restaurant," the Paradise also served Maine lobster and steak to satisfy more cautious tastes.

Youngsters growing up in small-town Asheville during those years remember the Paradise Restaurant as a place to see their chums. Said one native Ashevillean who's now about sixty years old, "The owner's children

Paradise Restaurant offered an exotic taste of Asian food. *North Carolina Collection, Pack Memorial Public Library, Asheville, North Carolina.*

were our age, so we grew up with them. When you went in, they would greet you like family. You felt like you were growing up with their family, and those kids were always in the restaurant."

At the Paradise Restaurant, for a change, food wasn't the usual fried chicken or biscuits and gravy. A meal was relatively cheap (a sixty-cent entrée included egg roll, rice and tea, with soup twenty cents extra), there was enough to feed the whole family and, well, it was nice to be greeted so warmly and served so graciously by the proprietor, Mr. Lee.

Thick Fon Lee came to America at age fourteen from Canton, China, arriving in Asheville in 1946 in his early thirties. A nephew and a brother of his ran the Paradise kitchen, and there may have been two other investors. Thick Fon Lee was the greeter. Regular customers received specially wrapped boxes of tea from him at Christmas, and children enjoyed Chinese candies. At Chinese New Year, he hosted elaborate ten-course banquets.

Mr. Lee's quiet dignity and his love of Chinese heritage commanded respect, and so did his actions. Formal elegance marked the furnishings, with Chinese embroideries adorning the walls.

His son, Roddy Lee, who later owned the Ming Tree restaurant on South Tunnel Road, once talked about his father: "My father basically lived at the restaurant. He worked there seven days a week from 10:30 a.m. until 11:30 or 12 o'clock at night." The restaurant was open 365 days a year.

"There was no such thing as vacations in our family. It was not until the late 1960s that he started closing one day for Christmas. My sister and I were in high school, and we talked him into it."

The local customer came first. When superstar Elvis Presley was in Asheville for an appearance in the city, he tried to rent the Paradise Restaurant for a private party—but Mr. Lee said no, his regular customers would be disappointed if they couldn't come in for dinner.

Yet tragedy touched the enterprise. In 1951, Eddie Lim, described at the time as an operator of Paradise Restaurant, received a ransom demand from Chinese Communists back home for the release of his mother, who had been unable to emigrate with the rest of the family. As an Asheville newspaper reported the chilling episode, unless Eddie Lim and his relatives came up with the equivalent of $2,000, she would be roasted alive.

"The mother, a woman in her sixties, given only enough food and water to keep her alive," was held under guard with no way to raise her own ransom, according to the coverage.

"Lim said last night that the family would not send money to the Reds.… 'We are worried.…We know that we cannot save her.'" Newspaper coverage did not mention the incident again.

Chinese friends in Knoxville had lost their father the same way.

Life for Asheville's immigrant restaurateurs took courage and stamina. In 1954, Mr. Lee survived a lead pipe attack during a robbery attempt at his restaurant. Later, son Roddy Lee retired from his own Ming Tree

LOST RESTAURANTS OF ASHEVILLE

restaurant at age forty, having worked in the restaurant business since age twelve.

In 1999, the Paradise Restaurant building sold for $151,000 and was swept up in Asheville's downtown renaissance. Today it houses Wasabi Japanese Restaurant.

THICK FON LEE DIDN'T BELIEVE American cooks could properly produce Chinese dishes without the right ingredients. However, in 1963, he felt comfortable sharing a recipe for what he called "egg fu young."

"This is a wonderful recipe to have," touted the *Asheville Citizen-Times*, "since it will use left-over meat, and is economical, very nourishing, highly nutritious, and not fattening." Note the lard.

Mr. Lee's "Egg Fu Young"

Dice meat, which may be chicken, ham, shrimp, pork or beef, cooked. Chop onions, mix with bean sprouts. Mix vegetables with the diced meat in about equal proportions.

Lightly beat four eggs, enough for one serving. Add the other ingredients to the egg, enough to give taste to the egg but not so much the egg cannot bind the mixture together.

Heat lard or a vegetable shortening in a skillet (the type used for frying chicken).

The egg fu young is cooked like pancakes, with three cakes to a serving. Ladle out enough of the batter for one cake and pour it carefully into the hot grease. When the cake is lightly brown, turn with spatula or pancake turner and remove instantly when done.

Serve with any gravy, adding soy sauce if desired.

CHAPTER 10

Tastee Diner

The NASCAR Effect

Welcome to West Asheville.

The story of Tastee Diner, opened in 1946 and still open after a 2016 reboot, is the story of West Asheville. Once upon a time, West Asheville was a separate town from today's sprawling City of Asheville, which is shaped like an elongated X about twelve miles north to south and nearly fourteen miles east to west.

West Asheville had its own history, not based on the livestock and stagecoach routes of the early 1800s that ran through Asheville's hilly downtown but on a mineral spring resort, Sulphur Springs, that was popular from about 1830 to 1893, situated at the western side of today's downtown West Asheville. Two hotels built one after the other at the same place, the Sulphur Springs Hotel and the Belmont, served the myriad health-conscious visitors who streamed in for therapeutic treatments. Both hotels eventually burned down, as structures lighted by candles were apt to do before modern fire safety.

The village that sprang up at Sulphur Springs had "farmers, two stores, four churches, a boarding house, and one lawyer." Livery stables and horses were big business well into twentieth-century Asheville and environs, and indeed Sulphur Springs had a half-mile racetrack for both trotting and running horses, called Carrier's, with bookmakers posting odds before each race.

The town of West Asheville was incorporated in 1884 (or 1889), by which time there was a bridge across the French Broad River and railroad service to

Sulphur Springs Hotel. Later unincorporated, West Asheville incorporated again from 1913 to 1917, and then by town vote it was annexed to Asheville.

West Asheville had a distinctive look and feel. It was an idyllic small blue-collar town on the road west to the great frontier. Built mostly at one time by one man, Edwin Carrier, West Asheville had a low-slung, unified profile along its main street—called Haywood Road—which was lined with shops and churches; the residential streets radiating from Haywood Road featured bungalows with small front yards and long, sloping backyards.

Clerks, factory hands, domestic workers, shopkeepers, mechanics—West Asheville was all about the common man. Churchgoing folks. During Asheville's up-and-down trajectory in the twentieth century, West Asheville also had its ups and downs. But there was always the Tastee Diner, at 575 Haywood Road, where local workers and retirees knew they could get breakfast, lunch or dinner, starting at 6:00 a.m. every day.

Local historian and preacher's kid Dan Pierce described his beloved town: "When I lived in West Asheville in the 1960 and '70s, it was a community colored by…red necks, white socks and blue ribbon beer,'" he wrote in the *Asheville Citizen-Times*. "Options for dining out in West Asheville were pretty limited, with the Tastee Diner about the only restaurant on Haywood Road."

Tastee Diner in West Asheville—old school. *North Carolina Collection, Pack Memorial Public Library, Asheville, North Carolina.*

After describing the many social institutions in West Asheville—church, Boy Scouts, fraternal organizations, stock car races—he continued: "We were mostly what you would today call 'free-range.' I now feel pretty privileged to have come from a place where gritty mill town met Mayberry, where stock car and baseball legends were made, and where working-class people struggled to give their children a better life and mostly did."

In its first sixty-five years, the Tastee Diner had only three sets of owners, starting with Morris and Grace Brown, who opened the place in what had been half of a commercial garage. Then came Sam and Margaret Evans, Tastee Diner's grill cook and waitress, respectively; that lasted until 1988 or '89, when steelworker David Hinson bought it so he could run his own place instead of working in a factory. All those owners treated the simple country menu and the faithful customers with love and respect. Some diners ate there every day for decades, so the staff knew just what to serve them, and when.

Tastee Diner – West Asheville, NC – May 2000   **Dan Lobdell**

Inside the old Tastee Diner in West Asheville. *North Carolina Collection, Pack Memorial Public Library, Asheville, North Carolina.*

"It wasn't broke, so we didn't try to fix it," Hinson told the *Citizen-Times* when he took over. "We've added some things as we've gone along, but mostly we've kept everything the same, because it works. Bacon and eggs, biscuits and gravy and the meat-and-three blue plate specials. The stuff people grew up with." He could have mentioned liver mush, bologna, meatloaf, catfish, beef stew, cooked apples and big fluffy western omelets.

What Hinson added to Tastee Diner was a NASCAR sensibility, with memorabilia honoring the grit of stock car drivers, like the ones who competed at West Asheville's New Asheville Speedway (long ago an air strip, now a bicycle track) or at the Asheville-Weaverville Speedway, an oval half-mile track. Such a racer would be the great Richard Petty, who in 1965 won the WNC 500—five hundred grueling laps of that dirt track—in a bit over three hours in his new Plymouth hemi.

"They're just down-home," Hinson said of his revered drivers in 1999. "We all started out with nothing. We're all just alike. No matter who they are or where you sit, you still feel they're your neighbor, whether you like them or not."

And there were similarities between NASCAR and religion. As historian Dan Pierce said, "Races always opened with prayer, folks had their regular seats at the track just like folks had their regular pews at church, and drivers even passed collection plates (their helmets) to help those in need."

As the years rolled on, Tastee Diner hardly changed. Same menu, shorter hours and, as West Asheville weathered years of decay, the same customers. Then something different happened. As downtown Asheville became popular, it became more expensive, and suddenly, around 2010, West Asheville real estate started looking like the land of opportunity. Investors moved in, young families moved in, lots of hip new restaurants moved in.

In 2016, Hinson sold the business to a restaurateur, Jonathan Robinson, whose high-end The Admiral put West Asheville on the culinary map. He and a partner reworked Tastee Diner as a "dairy bar throwback," modernizing the menu and the prices.

These days, West Asheville is upbeat, with new parents, retirees and an astonishingly varied immigrant community all calling the place home. And now there's a new version of Tastee Diner in the same location. It's open seven days a week, 8:00 a.m. to 9:00 p.m., with a menu of burgers, fried stuff and sweets. And kimchi.

In fact, the new-old atmosphere at Tastee Diner is a weird and wonderful mix. The aroma of bacon—the decades-old aroma of bacon—seems as ancient as the paint, the bar stools and the old tables. But the addition of

Above: Tastee Diner, under new management. *Photo by Nan K. Chase.*

Left: Tastee Diner's new sign. *Photo by Nan K. Chase.*

happy hour—even happy hour ice cream cones—brings in all sorts of up-to-date beverages and new drinkers. The staff is young—androgynous, pierced, tattooed and friendly. Gone are the NASCAR decorations, for the most part, which have been replaced with lots of fascinating photos of mid-twentieth-century Asheville.

It's worth a visit for the superb peach milkshake.

CHAPTER 11

Peterson's Grill

Family Comes First

Consider the word *delicatessen*. It means "delicacies": cooked meats, prepared salads, specialty dishes to eat in a restaurant or take home. Savor, then, the delicatessen-rich menu from the last day of business at Peterson's Grill, an institution on North Pack Square for thirty years that closed on October 31, 1977. Peterson's Grill was a family business that epitomized the twentieth-century immigrant experience and characterized the impact of Asheville's close-knit Greek community on the city's restaurant scene. At Peterson's Grill, kosher meats and country ham got equal billing—just like America, all mixed up together, something for everyone.

Sandwiches? They numbered in the dozens, including goose liver with lettuce and tomato, beef tongue with mustard and pickle, deviled egg sandwich or stuffed olive sandwich, hot salami and egg sandwich, kosher or Italian salami sandwich and plain old peanut butter and jelly. Reportedly, hams were sometimes air-cured in an open window of the back kitchen.

Then there were "Peterson's Famous Combinations," mind-bending sandwiches like "Swiss Cheese, Goose Liver, Baked Ham, Salami," or "Tongue and Swiss Cheese," or "Sliced Chicken and Goose Liver," or the Dr. Feldman Special, which consisted of "corned beef, smoked tongue, Swiss cheese, lettuce, and tomato."

Almost a dozen different cold plates—Peterson's Famous Cold Plates—were those same meats served with potato salad, sliced tomatoes, pickles and olives, rather than on bread.

There was more. Steaks and chops, roast chicken (with notorious bright yellow gravy), "knackwurst," leg of lamb, roast turkey with dressing, veal, broiled calf liver, chicken giblets and other meat-and-two-vegetable entrées; stewed oysters or oysters in the shell, deviled crabs, fried scallops and clams; chicken liver omelets, oyster omelets, brain omelets, onion omelets and jelly omelets. The array of seafood cold platters hinted at the owners' Greek heritage: choice of domestic or imported sardines, shrimp platter or tuna. There was Greek salad or simply a serving of feta cheese. In 1977, a western T-bone steak topped out the price range at four dollars.

For drinkers, the taproom offered beer and wine, plus two sizes of sherry and two kinds of port. For non-drinkers, a half pint of "cream buttermilk" cost twenty-five cents. Dessert was noteworthy: half a dozen different pies, plus homemade strawberry shortcake and peach cobbler.

Peterson's had it all, serving customers from 5:00 a.m. to midnight every day. The hard work and long hours—the faith and hope—that the owners devoted to their family enterprise were facts of life. "You Don't Have to Be Rich to Eat at PETERSON'S," read one early advertisement that described it simply as "Asheville's Reasonably Priced Restaurant."

The Peterson family wasn't looking to get rich, necessarily, just seeking to join the American middle class. "They had to borrow money during the slow winter season and paid it back during the good summer trade with enough extra to call it a good living," a newspaper account recalled.

In the 1950s, in a move to increase cash flow, Peterson's Grill bid for the contract to feed Asheville's prisoners housed in the jail nearby, losing one year's bid by a penny a meal and another year splitting the contract with a competitor. For thirty-five cents a meal—two meals a day, since breakfast was black coffee at seven cents a cup—Peterson's provided meat, vegetable sides and tea to drink.

Peterson's Grill had its origins about two generations before it actually opened at 10 North Pack Square in 1947. Greek immigrants had begun settling around Asheville soon after 1900, when much of the downtown was still a "mud hole" with only rudimentary public services. Sidewalks were wooden planks laid over knee-deep mire. But demand for food was high, and working in cafés and restaurants quickly became a favored career. A stream of countrymen followed from the mountains of Greece, bringing with them a ferocious work ethic, deeply religious ways, devotion to family and a belief in American democracy—all valued traits in western North Carolina.

In 1927, an immigrant named Gus Peterson opened the Asheville Lunch Room, or possibly Asheville Quick Lunch, on Patton Avenue. With his

Busy Pack Square was home to many eating establishments, including Peterson's Grill. *North Carolina Collection, Pack Memorial Public Library, Asheville, North Carolina.*

brother Nick, he then purchased Vick's Grill at 66 Haywood Street. In a random twist of branding, the neon sign for Vick's couldn't be changed easily to Haywood Grill—the Petersons' preferred name—because of shortages of neon gas. So Vick's got changed to Nick's.

The two Peterson brothers did well enough, and eventually each had two sons. The four younger Petersons left home to serve in World War II and came back hoping to become professionals in other fields. But the aging uncles needed them to continue the business for the family's sake. So they stayed, in 1947 rebranding Nick's Grill as Peterson's Grill and moving it to the North Pack Square location.

Enter Akzona.

By the mid-1970s, Asheville's central commercial district, once so dynamic that crowds of shoppers spilled off the sidewalks, was cored out. Dead. The first suburban shopping mall had come to town in 1956, and after that, downtown slid into a desperate decline, exacerbated by the city's near bankruptcy in 1930 and the travails that followed.

The Dutch textile firm Enka—for Eerste Nederlandsche Kunstzjidefabriek Arnhem—already operated a rayon factory west of Asheville and had brought with it progressive business practices. Enka

Peterson's Grill and other businesses before the Akzona Building. *North Carolina Collection, Pack Memorial Public Library, Asheville, North Carolina.*

was subsumed into Akzona Inc., and in 1977, when Akzona proposed building its new corporate headquarters in downtown Asheville, the reception was enthusiastic.

Enka wanted to buy an entire city block, consisting of six commercial buildings dating from the late 1800s. Peterson's Grill occupied one of them. Those buildings were badly aged, and the Peterson cousins took Akzona's buyout offer. The six buildings came down, and in their place rose the half-mirrored, ship-like structure commissioned from architect I.M. Pei. Ironically, Akzona was soon out of business, but that modern anchor helped jump-start Asheville's twenty-first-century downtown renaissance anyway. Since 1986, the building has housed Biltmore corporate headquarters.

When Peterson's Grill closed, its tribute included these words from the *Asheville Citizen*: "Peterson's Grill presented the illusion that time had stopped there….It was a frozen specimen of time, too new to be historic, too old to be rescued from the inevitability of events."

CHAPTER 12

Swiss Kitchen

"Worth Yodeling About!"

Emile and Margaret Eberle certainly weren't shy. They often proclaimed that their Swiss Kitchen, which operated on Hendersonville Road from the mid-1940s until 1969, was "Worth Yodeling About!"

The jaunty advertisements for Swiss Kitchen touted food "as high as the Alps in quality," lunchtime sandwiches "Hearty for the men, Dainty for the ladies, Memorable for both" and "TASTE, CLEANLINESS, and an air of informal charm [that] combine to give you that 'PEACE WITH THE WORLD' feeling." Phew, not bad for a restaurant.

There was an enthusiastic, educational slant to the Eberles' ads, too. "Did you ever taste Ramequins?…Gnetschlets?…Swiss Salad Bowl?" "If You Only Knew What We Prepared for You!" What they prepared was everything. "Yes, and Real Western Steaks, Southern Fried Chicken with HUSHPUPPIES (none better)…all rolls and pastries home-made, of course."

Of course.

With its rich menu, costumed waiters and waitresses and cozy wood-paneled dining room bedecked with baskets of geraniums—well, no wonder Swiss Kitchen could brag that it was "unique within 500 miles." The establishment projected its owners' warmth and sense of cultural pride.

The Swiss Kitchen, in a word, radiated joy. The joy of eating fresh, wholesome foods prepared with love, exactitude and a light hand on the

Sunday- August 17, 1952

SWISS KITCHEN

Tasty Foods

WORTH YODELING ABOUT!

TRADE MARK

Phone 2-1462

Mr. and Mrs. E. G. Eberle,
Proprietors

Did you ever taste Ramequins?

... Gnetschlets? ... Swiss Salad Bowl?
yes, and Real Western Steaks, Southern Fried
Chicken with HUSHPUPPIES (none better)
... all rolls and pastries home-made, of
course ...

DINE WITH US!
for these and other fine Swiss and American
foods.

Breakfast: 8:00 - 9:00 A. M.
Luncheon: 11:00 A. M. - 2:00 P. M.
Dinner: 5:00 - 9:30 P. M.
And Sandwiches ... Hearty for the men,
Dainty for the ladies, Memorable for both ...
with soft drinks ... served 'till 5:00 P. M.
—Private Parties on Advance Reservations—

U. S. 25 (Hendersonville Rd.) ASHEVILLE, N. C.

TASTE, CLEANLINESS, and an air of informal charm combine to give you that "PEACE
WITH THE WORLD" feeling. Comfortable lounge chairs and umbrellas on lawn are available for after-dining relaxation.

Recommended by DUNCAN HINES

A postcard promotes Swiss Kitchen. *North Carolina Collection, Pack Memorial Public Library,
Asheville, North Carolina.*

spices. Swiss cuisine, the Eberles instructed prospective customers in their
crisp display ads, was similar to German but not as heavy, similar to French
but not as "sauce-y" yet with "the robust touch of Italian fare."

"And, of course, dairy products are a vital part of the food of a land
known for its pastures and herds and farms."

Of course.

The Eberles were intimately involved with every aspect of their
restaurant, and menus reflected their rare sensibility for fine dining. Yet
prices remained moderate.

For example, an early Special Sunday Dinner began at "The Beginning—
Ramequins of Herring in Sour Cream." Then came chicken rice soup,
followed by Baked Ham in Wine Sauce with Golden Brown Apple Fritters."
Yum. Then, broccoli or cream carrots, pineapple salad with Swiss Kitchen
salad dressing and, finally, Swiss Apple Tarts or Eberle Swiss Cake. Oh, yes,
homemade clover leaf rolls and a beverage, of course. "Cost: $2.00."

Another two-dollar Sunday dinner gave a hint of Mrs. Eberle's
culinary skills. One heavenly dessert was named Eberle Swiss Cake with
Brandy Cream.

The restaurant's setting helped its popularity. Swiss Kitchen—sometimes
called Swiss Kitchen Lodge—occupied a handsome chalet that had been
known as Whitehall Lodge, once home to the Starnes family and precisely

A bucolic setting for Swiss Kitchen. *North Carolina Collection, Pack Memorial Public Library, Asheville, North Carolina.*

five miles south of Asheville's Pack Square. The building had an outdoor dining patio and was surrounded by an expansive lawn, and beyond that lay thick woods. In those days, the location was well out of town, but the city has expanded, and today Hendersonville Road rolls on for another six miles southward beyond that spot before it leaves the city limits.

And there was more to the Swiss Kitchen than just dining. "In addition to serving fabulous meals, the Swiss Kitchen also operates a large mailing business for cheeses and other goodies, Mrs. Eberle's own cakes, küchen and Swiss cake," a newspaper reported in 1963.

"The küchen she has adapted from authentic family recipes into a loaf which can be sliced and toasted, thus making it something to dream about. There is also a gift shop where carefully chosen and exquisite jewelry, Portuguese pottery, and items from other foreign and exotic lands are available. Mr. Eberle manages and buys for the shop."

In their own advertisements, the Eberles went further. Sales of merchandise at their "Swiss Museum of Gifts" amounted to a "paramount cultural event."

Generally, Swiss Kitchen was open from May through late October, with the gift shop reopening in early winter for holiday shopping.

Breakfast, when offered, was a spare one hour, 8:00 to 9:00 a.m. (no Monday service), luncheon from 11:00 a.m. to 2:00 p.m. and dinner from 5:00 to 9:30 p.m.

Swiss Kitchen's aesthetic also ran along strict racial lines. Help-wanted ads were specific: "Swiss Kitchen Lodge wants three clean, wholesome refined white waitresses. Also colored male or female cook." Or "colored salad girl with experience," "colored baker helper," "bus boy. White. Alert and neat," "White boys apply in person," "White or colored baker helper" and "Want college students for pleasant summer jobs." Because Swiss Kitchen was seasonal, staying open only part of each year, the frequent help-wanted ads provide a window into business operations.

Swiss Kitchen ended suddenly. By October 1, 1969, the Eberles had closed up for good and were living in Georgia, according to a news account. Exactly four weeks later, a fire started in the restaurant's basement in the middle of the night. Nearly thirty firefighters fought to bring the blaze under control, and damage was extensive.

Today, the site is a suburban shopping center

In 1961, the *Asheville Citizen-Times* published several mouthwatering recipes from the Swiss Kitchen, including Swiss Roesti Potatoes and Hazelnut Bars. These savory ramequins have countless variations. The Zwieble Waya is an onion pie, much like quiche.

Swiss Ramequins or Zwieble Waya

Line tart shells with a good pie dough.

Mix together for each shell, two tablespoonsful of very finely grated imported Swiss cheese and two tablespoonsful of Gruyere cheese and sprinkle into the shell. Add ¼ teaspoonful of grated onion.

Filling for six tart shells: 1½ cups of coffee cream, three eggs beaten together, a pinch of salt. Beat lightly together. Use to fill the tart shells, pouring carefully over the cheese layer.

Bake in 375 degree oven until light brown.

Serve hot or cold.

In little tart shells, the recipe makes delightful appetizers.

For the Zwieble Waya, prepare one large pie shell (9-inch) and use the quantity of grated cheeses that would be used for six tarts.

Instead of grating onion, slice very thinly and place over the cheese; include also cubed cooked ham, or broken pieces of crisp bacon. Then pour the egg-cream mixture, in quantities listed above for six tart shells. Addition of ham or bacon and more onion makes a wonderful lunch "pie," served with a crisp green salad and crusty bread.

CHAPTER 13

Rabbit's

"Beacon of Pride"

I magine Asheville in the 1940s, with racial segregation creating two cities: one black, one white. Rabbit's Tourist Court, which included the famous "soul-food stronghold" known simply as Rabbit's, was part of the former. Here was an establishment where the "Negro" traveling public, as well as generations of local residents, could relax, dine and stay the night without the sting of "a welt on their self-esteem" inflicted by social exclusion, as writer Susan Reinhardt put it in an *Asheville Citizen-Times* column.

Louella Byrd, a relative of Rabbit's founder, said simply, "You couldn't eat in a white-run restaurant. There was nowhere for black people to go."

And so it was that Rabbit's was the sort of place that *The Negro Motorist Green Book* could include. That directory, which appeared from 1936 to 1966, was better known by its nickname, *The Green Book*, after its publisher, Victor H. Green.

At Rabbit's, the pork chops were "as thick as Bibles," according to one admiring reviewer in 1995, during the diner's last decade of business. And that was just one item on a menu that featured "truly amazing home cooking at astoundingly low prices."

Everything was mouthwatering: fried chicken that was "juicy and tender" inside yet "crackling on the outside," collard greens boiled long and slow to meld the flavors, catfish, chitlins, candied yams, pinto beans, mashed potatoes and gravy, cabbage and squash casserole. And dessert. Wine and beer were served, but the selection was limited; the only wine available was white wine, and the only beers were Bud, Bud Ice and Michelob Light. Even

R & G Grocery (Mrs Evelyn B Rice) 1448 Merrimon av

RABBIT'S TOURIST COURT (FRED SIMP-SON), A COLORED TOURIST COURT WITH RESTAURANT, 110 McDOWELL, TEL 9624

Rabie Walter M (Lillie) boiler opr Gennett Flooring Co h Thompson

Listing for Rabbit's Motor Court in the *Green Book*. *North Carolina Collection, Pack Memorial Public Library, Asheville, North Carolina.*

into the twenty-first century, Rabbit's pegged dinner at seven dollars or less—a bargain. Cash only.

In the year 2000, another review of Rabbit's described the experience:

> *The ribs were succulent and rich and flavored all the way through rather than bland inside like so many are. The fried pork chops were large, crisp, golden and delicious and the (huge) chicken breast was done just right....*
>
> *But the side dishes were the real stars of the meal—it would be easy to make a complete dinner of these, accompanied only by a slab of homemade cornbread. The green beans and squash were delicious, the macaroni and cheese was to die for, the black-eyed peas were amazing but the collard greens...were the best any of us had ever had.*

Rabbit's seemed to inspire Asheville restaurant reviewers to new heights of prose. Macaroni and cheese was "macaroni smothered under a carpet of cheese," while cornbread emerged from the oven "cracking open and running with butter, a meal in itself sponged with a glass of buttermilk."

Rabbit's was the creation of Fred Simpson, nicknamed Rabbit for his running speed. It opened in 1947 or 1948 with a neon sign of a rabbit with legs in motion and closed sometime in the early 2000s. The old Rabbit's property, long abandoned, nowadays may be headed for an interesting rebirth.

The location, at 110 McDowell Street, near today's large Mission Health hospital complex, was initially part of Asheville's center city black residential and business community called Southside (today's brewpub zone), and the diner managed to hold fast to its niche even as McDowell Street was widened and turned into a strip of doctors' offices and medical

Rabbit's had dining and lodging options. *Photo by Peggy Gardener, North Carolina Collection, Pack Memorial Public Library, Asheville, North Carolina.*

clinics. The family that operated Rabbit's fended off repeated entreaties to sell the property for redevelopment.

Descriptions of the place vary significantly. At first, the motel and diner were upscale, according to an account by SoundSpace@Rabbit's, the new music rehearsal space and soul food café that was slated to open on the ruins of the old Rabbit's in 2019 (that timetable proved to be overly optimistic).

> *Rabbit's Tourist Court was a crown jewel of Negro "Tourist Courts" for Negro travelers in the south, and was an $85,000 business at its opening....Its decorative dining room boasted an indoor fountain; its kitchen was ultra-modern and stocked, and its motel cabins elegant and handsome. The white stone driveway was light[ed] with red, blue and yellow lights, and had curb service from its restaurant.*

Can that be the same restaurant later described in downscale terms like "quietly faded"? One longtime customer said, "Walking in the front door you take a step back in time into a small room with linoleum floors, fake brick siding and formica tables and booths, each with its own vase of

Rabbit's Tourist Court. *Andrea Clark Photograph Collection, North Carolina Collection, Pack Memorial Public Library, Asheville, North Carolina.*

fake flowers....There's nothing outside the building to tell people there's good food inside, only a sign reading 'Rabbit's Motel.' But somehow word gets around."

In Rabbit's later years, the diner offered lunch service in addition to dinner and hired chef Robert Livingston to modernize the menu by lightening calorie counts and adding baked items to fried fare. Still, the run was over, and Rabbit's Motel and the restaurant succumbed to the elements.

An exciting new development holds promise, however. With fundraising possibly underway but the broken-down buildings still to be cleared from the old Rabbit's lot, two young entrepreneurs and a culinary expert related to the Rabbit's founder want to tap the music and dining scene swirling nearby. "We are honoring this legacy by creating a cultural landmark with building murals, and a new soul food café," they say on their website, soundspaceavl.com.

THE *ASHEVILLE CITIZEN-TIMES* PUBLISHED TWO of Rabbit's "gourmet soul food" recipes, courtesy of chef Ronald Livingston:

Apple Cinnamon Pork Chops

2 pork chops weighing between 4 and 6 ounces
½ cup sugar
½ cup water
⅓ cup heavy whipping cream
⅓ cup mascarpone (an Italian cream cheese)
1 tablespoon sour cream
¼ to ½ red apple cut into wedges
Cinnamon to taste

Grill, fry, bake or otherwise prepare the pork chops how you like them.
Over medium heat, combine the water, sugar, whipping cream, cheese, sour cream and cinnamon. Bring to a boil, stirring constantly, then reduce heat. Add apple wedges, cover and let thicken, stirring occasionally. Sauce is ready when the apple wedges are softened. Ladle over pork chops.

Collard Greens

3 to 4 bunches of collard greens
1 ½ cups of water
2 ham hocks
(All of the following are to taste)
Fatback
Bacon drippings
Seasoning salt
Black pepper
Garlic powder (not garlic salt)
Pinch of sugar
Dash of white vinegar

Tear the collard greens (Livingston recommends trying the Farmers Market) from their stems. Wash the leaves until there's no grit or sand left in the bottom of the sink. Shake dry (don't use a salad spinner).
Add all the ingredients and bring the water to a brisk boil. Reduce to a medium boil and cover. Stir occasionally. Cook until tender, about an hour and a half. Serves 15.

CHAPTER 14

Hillbilly Rest-Runt

The Real McCoy

The Hillbilly Rest-Runt was offensive in so many ways.

First, the name. The word "hillbilly" was galling enough to some people, let alone the use of "rest-runt" instead of "restaurant."

Second, the company's advertisements, which aped mountain people by depicting them as gap-toothed, barefoot and clothed in rags (with lots of raggedy barefoot children) and by misspelling half the words and writing many of the letters backward. "Why sakes erlive! We un's hev got a passel uf food out at our place 'n jist itching to wait on the likes of you—hand and foot—cum on out!" read a newspaper ad for the grand opening in late June 1951.

Finally, the entertainment. Although Hillbilly Rest-Runt actually had a spacious new dance floor with room for at least a five-piece orchestra, the restaurant boasted that a popular Georgia act called Aunt Fanny's Cabin Kids would be making its rounds through the dining room. These were the same "young—very young—Negro singers" who had performed at a plantation-themed restaurant called Aunt Fanny's Cabin near Atlanta, Georgia, singing the menu and carrying a menu board "just in case they are not understood" and presenting such "appropriately Southern numbers" as "The South Will Rise Again."

Bad, bad, bad.

And yet…

And yet, Hillbilly Rest-Runt was paying strange, tone-deaf homage to one of the most resourceful and tenacious groups of people to live near

Hillbilly Rest-Runt advertisement. *North Carolina Collection, Pack Memorial Public Library, Asheville, North Carolina.*

Asheville: the mountain folk who had settled the rugged backwoods and learned to forage, hunt and preserve—"put up"—nearly everything they needed to survive.

Indeed, today's edible wild food movement owes a debt to the so-called hillbillies, who purchased little more than coffee beans (green, to roast at home), salt and sugar. Everything else necessary for a nutritious and flavorful diet came from the woods or from small clearings they tended: nuts, berries, herbs, grains, vegetables and greens. They made their own medicines and their own pleasures; imagine tucking into hot biscuits spread with geranium butter or quince honey. Hillbilly homemakers had recipes for cooking bear, squirrel, grouse, wild turkey, venison, rabbit, muskrat, raccoon, crawfish, groundhog, turtle, possum and frog, as well as for vinegar pie, mushroom catsup and purslane casserole.

The man who created the Hillbilly Rest-Runt was no rube, and in fact, once the initial flurry of hillbilly-themed advertising was over, he settled into a more sophisticated tone.

Harvey Hester was a local fellow, a football star in college and a highly decorated combat veteran of World War I. It was Hester who created Aunt Fanny's Cabin in Smyrna, Georgia, and ran it for nearly twenty years. He wanted to apply a similar wink-wink decorative motif to an Asheville operation.

His cartoonish ad copy for the June 29, 1951 grand opening told the story, with many reversed letters, of course: "An eating place thet Asheville has bin waiting fer! Harvey Hester, operator of that 'Aunt Fanny's Cabin,' nationally known fer it's grand food, is opening another ol' place here in Asheville. He has done gone the limit on hillbilly decoratuns, the likez of which you've never seen an the food is the likes of which us hillbilly hav never seen!"

Hester seems to have considered himself a fellow hillbilly but too clever by half. In the same grand opening advertisement, he admitted that he had "done such a complete job of burlesquing the hillbilly that even us mountain folks have done got eshamed of our trifling ways."

His "hillbilly decoratuns" included an "actual pig pen" on the roof garden—called the Barnyard Roof—and "humorous hillbilly cartoons everwhurs." Those cartoons, in fact, were murals painted by Atlanta artist Vaughn Stewart.

Hester's vision, according to grand opening newspaper coverage, was to welcome big-city visitors to the mountains with an informality that would help them relax while on vacation. "Hester has gone all out to make his Rest-Runt a place that will appeal both to their humor and their desire for fine food."

For when all was said and done, the Hillbilly Rest-Runt was not about groundhog stew or boiled dandelion greens. It was about chipped beef with mushroom sauce, filet of sole, salmon croquettes, broiled chicken and leg of lamb with mint jelly, all served with vegetables in season and fresh-baked goods.

Located about four miles east of Asheville's Pack Square, at 1085 Tunnel Road in the Oteen section, the restaurant was open for breakfast, lunch and dinner and open all day on Sunday.

Despite Hester's best efforts, Hillbilly Rest-Runt didn't thrive. Five months after opening, he filed a bankruptcy petition, owing $17,000 to vendors and another $4,000 in federal cabaret tax. He seems to have righted the operation for a while, but by the mid-1950s, it was failing; the target market pivoted from tourists to "business men" and "career girls."

The "rotund" Hester died in 1967.

"Good Food, Good Fun, Good Entertainment, Good Everything," his ads had promised. Maybe not so much.

FOLK REMEDIES

Compiled for Appalachian Recipes *by the Kentuckiana Buckhorn Alumni Association, 1976*

For burns:
"The scrapings of a raw white potato will draw the fire."

For colds:
"Drink red pepper tea."
"Drink tea made from wintergreen fern."
"Eat onions roasted in ashes."

To stop bleeding:
"Place a spider web across the wound."
"Use a mixture of soot from the chimney and lard."

RECIPES FROM *SOUTHERN APPALACHIAN MOUNTAIN COOKIN'* BY LOUISE AND BIL DWYER

Granny's Sack Dumperlin'

Make a sack of unbleached muslin. Dip sack in boiling water. Remove and coat the inside with flour. Mix 1 quart blackberries, 1 cup flour, ½ teaspoon baking powder, and salt and sugar to taste. Put mixture into sack and tie tightly with a string. Drop into boiling water for one hour. Turn out of sack and serve with cream.

Fried Cucumbers

Pare 2 cucumbers, then cut in slices about ¼ inch thick. Pat dry with a towel. Dip each slice in fine dry bread crumbs, then beaten egg, then again in the crumbs. Fry a few at a time in deep fat. When slices are golden brown, drain on paper. Season with salt and pepper.

CHAPTER 15

Bucks, Wink's and Babe Maloy's

The Big Three

World War II ended in August 1945, and even though the United States and its allies had prevailed in the conflict, American society itself was now poised on the edge of a revolution that would play out over the next few decades. But in the first exhilarating postwar years, it would be nearly impossible to see those changes ahead, the cracks in the foundation, the seismic shifts between the races and the sexes that would fracture the cultural landscape. It was as though Americans were about to build an amusement park on a volcano.

There was pent-up economic demand after the sacrifices that had gone into full wartime production. Housing, cars, appliances, clothes and cosmetics, tourism and recreation—everything had been put on hold to turn out bombers and bullets, to equip and feed the 16 million American men and women who served in the war effort, by one estimate more than 10 percent of the country's 140 million population at the time. And there was ground to be made up following the Great Depression of the 1930s, which had wracked the nation before the war and helped empty the countryside.

There were postwar demographic changes as the soldiers returned home and quickly started families, leading to the baby boom. While the economy settled into growth mode, there was plenty of work to go around. By the early 1950s, a new generation of teenagers had part-time jobs after school and on weekends, with change jingling in their pockets. They had cars, they had freedom (the white kids anyway) and they wanted to have fun. "Drive-happy teens," local historian Rob Neufeld called them in a fifty-year retrospective published in the *Asheville Citizen-Times* in 2017. Go, go, go. Everyone was on the go, and thanks to the new interstate highway system they could go farther, faster.

The time was ripe for the advent of the drive-in, a new kind of restaurant where customers didn't even get out of their cars; the food came to them. After all, who had time to cook elaborate meals, especially in communities like Asheville where domestic help long had been a mainstay…but no longer was. The dinner table, once the center of American home life, began to lose its grip on the family.

In Asheville, three drive-in restaurants that operated in the thirty years after the war are fondly recalled by that generation of teens now in their sunset years. These drive-ins were known as the Big Three: Bucks, Wink's and Babe Maloy's. Clustered near one another on Tunnel Road, they were considered a single entity, a triangular circuit for social cruising, for seeing and being seen. Local writer Barbara Blake called Tunnel Road a "neon mecca."

Far from being just places where friends could gather for burgers and milkshakes, the Big Three drive-ins were riding the wave of social change, and the men who founded those establishments were movers and shakers in the development of Asheville's now-epic tourism economy; they were friends with one another, and they invested everything in their city's success. For them, drive-ins weren't just for fun—they were serious business. Eventually, of course, the drive-ins also became victims of larger economic forces in the United States.

BUCKS—USUALLY SPELLED WITH NO APOSTROPHE—WAS the first to open, on May 1, 1946. Newspaper histories of the place vary, with the name initially the Drive In Restaurant, then Bucks Restaurant, later becoming Bucks Drive-In or sometimes Bucks Famous Restaurant. No matter what it was called, Bucks was big stuff. There was seating for forty-seven indoors and plenty of parking. The "drive-in" moniker delineated the place from Asheville's downtown restaurants, where patrons usually parked and walked or took buses. After a decade in business, Bucks added its instantly popular curbside service.

Tourists had been making their way to Asheville for well over a century by then, as regular stagecoach service brought them up from the hot, malarial lowlands beginning in the early 1800s, prosperous visitors from South Carolina, Georgia and even New Orleans. Later, after rail service reached Asheville, in 1880, tourism exploded. Everyone, it seemed, wanted to enjoy the cool air and the fine scenery.

In 1927, as part of renowned city planner John Nolen's development outline for Asheville, blasting work began on Beaucatcher Tunnel to relieve the crush of traffic that had to thread its way by car over the last treacherous mountain passes into town, where visitors could spend money and have a good time. Once the tunnel was finished, in 1929, the road that had been known as Black Mountain Highway—coming into town from the east— morphed into Tunnel Road.

Today, that busy four-lane thoroughfare is lined with big-box stores, motels and franchise restaurants, but back when John O. "Buck" Buchanan bought land on the eastern side of the tunnel for a little more than $6,000, the area was nearly deserted. There was one motel and some cabins.

"We carved this place out of the woods," Buchanan told an *Asheville Citizen* reporter in 1972, repeating the story for another reporter in 1985. "This was a pine forest."

He wasn't a restaurant man yet, although by 1954, the North Carolina Association of Quality Restaurants named him Restaurateur of the Year. Buchanan had come to the Asheville area in 1932, running Buchanan's 5&10 in the nearby community of Swannanoa. A year later, he joined the shipping department of the Beacon Manufacturing Co. there, and he stayed employed for the next thirteen years, until he bought the Tunnel Road property and opened a restaurant. A different newspaper account had Buchanan in charge of the Beacon company canteen during the "slow years" of the 1930s, as well as operating a nightclub atop the Plaza Theatre, in downtown Asheville.

Buchanan's emphasis was on quality fare: "prime ribs, steaks, seafood and barbecue," as the *Asheville Citizen* recounted. "He worked on the assumption that people would pay good prices for quality food." And they did. Buchanan added catering to his business, and he took over the Florida Court Motel and changed the name to Bucks Motel. Eventually, Buchanan owned nine acres on Tunnel Road.

Thanks to Buchanan's vision, hard work and steady re-investment, his business took off. A recap in a 1964 edition of the *Asheville Citizen* detailed the upgrades to date:

> *1950—Expansion of the dining room and kitchen facilities.*
> *1954—More dining facilities and expanded curb service.*
> *1960—New curb service building, butcher and bake shops and cold storage.*
> *1962—Buck's Sirloin Room opened at Asheville Airport.*
> *1965—The Red Carpet Room.*

That upscale amenity called the Red Carpet Room, added to the drive-in, was fancy, a place where stars and dignitaries visiting Asheville would come. Actress Grace Kelly, the Reverend Billy Graham and boxers Jack Dempsey and Joe Louis all came to dine.

Local writer Carole Currie wrote in the *Citizen-Times* in 2016:

> *The crème de la crème of dining spots was Bucks on Tunnel Road. It shared the odd combination of a very popular drive-in food business with indoor dining including The Red Carpet Room. The Red Carpet Room was the destination for birthday, anniversary and special occasion dinners, and for us it was a rare treat.*
>
> *That was the place to go for a good steak and for the once ubiquitous gulf shrimp cocktail. Business deals were made there, and when celebrities came to town, it was to the Red Carpet Room they were taken.*

The bifurcated nature of Bucks, with the informal drive-in and the formal Red Carpet Room, was unusual, but it worked. At the height of Buchanan's mini-empire, the "vast, black-topped parking lot" could hold hundreds of cars at once, often with four teens to a car. Bob Terrell, a local observer writing for the Asheville newspapers, called it "the largest culinary complex in the state" and the most profitable "per volume." At its busiest, Bucks did $2 million in business a year.

Meanwhile, the drive-in culture got bigger and bigger along Tunnel Road, thanks to the hamburger.

What had begun in 1873 as the Hamburg steak, a specialty of New York City's famous Delmonico Steakhouse, met the concept of a sliced bread roll—the bun—around the time of the St. Louis World's Fair in 1904. (It was during the St. Louis fair that Grover Wolfe, a brother of Asheville's famous author Thomas Wolfe, died of typhoid fever while his mother ran a temporary rooming house there.) With condiments added, plus side servings of French fries and a soda or shake, the hamburger became an American institution—a meal on the run.

The Bucks 1954 menu featured the "Buckburger," made with Iowa beef. This treat had "2 Pure Beef Patties, Sliced Cheese, Red Ripe Tomato, Crisp Shredded Lettuce and Dill Chip." It was served on a toasted bun slathered with Bucks own Special Dressing. The price was fifty-five cents. A slightly bigger beef tenderloin on a bun, with all the sides, cost eighty-five cents. The sixty-five-cent Banquet in a Basket was basically a ham sandwich, but the Bucks prose went on and on:

The Red Carpet Room at Bucks. *North Carolina Collection, Pack Memorial Public Library, Asheville, North Carolina.*

"Delicious Hickory Smoked Virginia Ham Sandwich on Toasted Bun, sliced tomato, Iceberg Lettuce, Pickle and Olive and a generous portion of Golden Brown French Fries—Real good!"

One Asheville youngster, Deane Johnson Nesbitt, fondly recalled the importance of Bucks. "Going to Bucks in the 1950s and '60s you had a purpose, which was to be seen and to see who-was-who and what kind of car they had. You could visit other teens—and sometimes even switch cars—without having to make a date."

Bucks was the first stop on the nightly teen circuit in those days, then came Wink's and Babe Maloy's. Then back by Bucks.

Babe Maloy credited the civic-minded Buchanan with helping him get started in his own successful endeavor—and with helping the tourism business in western North Carolina take wing.

Buchanan saw everyone's businesses as connected to every other one and to the larger community as well. Success for one helped all the others succeed, at least when it came to tourism. He served on a long list of public boards and commissions: the city's housing authority, the chamber of commerce, a local country club board, a hospital board and the committee for improving the Asheville Civic Center, as well as the State Highway Commission, the North Carolina Board of Conservation and Development and the state Alcoholic Beverage Control Board. He was a club man, too, a Shriner, a Mason, a president of the Dad's Club, plus a student in a men's Bible class. He was a basketball and football booster for the University of North Carolina. "Serve others," he urged friends.

And in 1972, he was ready to retire. Buchanan sold Bucks Restaurant to Fred M. Walker and Bucks Motel to the Walker Corporation, but the

Special Sandwich Menu

"BUCKBURGER"

Made with 2 Pure Beef Patties, Sliced Cheese, Red Ripe Tomato, Crisp Shredded Lettuce and Dill Chip. Served with Bucks own Special Dressing on Toasted Bun—We're sure you'll like it! .55

BANQUET IN A BASKET

Delicious Hickory Smoked Virginia Ham Sandwich on Toasted Bun, sliced tomato, Iceberg Lettuce, Pickle and Olive and a generous portion of Golden Brown French Fries—Real good! .65

FROM THE GRILL

Beef Tenderloin, French Fries	.85
On toasted bun, lettuce, tomato	
Sliced Chicken, Lettuce and Tomato	.65
Pure Beef Hamburger	.30
Roast Beef or Pork, Sliced Tomato and Lettuce	.45
Kosher Corned Beef, Potato Chips	.85
On rye, dill pickle, deviled egg, cole slaw	
Fried Perch on Bun—Tartar Sauce	.35
Hickory Smoked Bar-B-Q, Beef or Pork	.45
Genuine Country Ham Sandwich, French Fries, sliced tomato, lettuce	.85
Sliced Chicken, bacon, lettuce and tomato	.75
Cheeseburger	.35
Grilled Cheese .30 Bacon, lettuce, tom.	.35
Hot Dog .20 Foot Long	.35
Special steak sandwich, lettuce, tomato	.45
Pan Boiled Chicken Livers	1.65
Buck's Special Combination Salad Bowl	.50
French, Roquefort or 1,000 Island Dressing	
French Fried Potatoes or Onion Rings served hot	.25

FROM THE FOUNTAIN

Thick malted with whipped cream	.35
Thick shakes .30 Sodas	.30
Above items in chocolate, vanilla and strawberry flavors	
Sundaes .30 With nuts	.35
Chocolate, cherry, pineapple	
Fresh Strawberry sundae	.35
Hot Fudge or Butterscotch Sundae	.35
Banana Split .40 Plain ice cream	.15
Home made pie .20 A La Mode	.30
Banana milk shake or malted	.35
Bucks Boston Cooler (Root Beer, Ice Cream)	.25
Coca-Cola .10 Lemonade	.15
Coffee, hot or iced tea	.10
Milk .12 Hot choc. or choc. milk	.15
Fresh Strawberry Shortcake, with ice cream—New	.50
Fresh Fruit Limeade, with Lime Sherbet	.25

A menu from the popular Bucks. *North Carolina Collection, Pack Memorial Public Library, Asheville, North Carolina.*

new owners quickly defaulted on their promissory notes. Buchanan took the restaurant back in 1974, spruced it up and ran it until 1976, when he sold it for an undisclosed sum to the Mom 'n Pop's company. Like so many other restaurant stories, this one has had a number of endings. Today, look for the site of Bucks where Olive Garden Italian Restaurant is located, at 121 Tunnel Road.

NEXT CAME WINK'S, IN 1950. By the time William and Richard A. "Jim" Winkenwerder opened their sleek drive-in at 17 Tunnel Road, teenage cruising was coming into full swing. The practice called "checking the drag" saw teenagers on their frequent circuit between Bucks, Wink's and Babe Maloy's. With fifty cents' worth of gas in the tank—sometimes pooled from several teens—there was no limit to the fun.

It was the age of cool, or at least of trying to look cool. For girls, that meant prim wraparound skirts or swirling poodle skirts worn with ankle socks and laced two-tone saddle shoes; demure blouses with rounded Peter Pan collars, cardigan sweaters, which were sometimes worn reversed with the buttons on the back; and carefully styled hair. Hair had to be just right: teased into towering beehives and kept in shape with a layer of hairspray or, if a girl had too-curly hair, ironed into submission on an ironing board. Such preparations could take an hour or more.

Boys were fine with an Elvis Presley–inspired uniform of dungarees or chinos with white socks, penny loafers, white T-shirts neatly tucked in and short sleeves rolled up to hold a pack of cigarettes and perhaps a dark leather jacket. Hair—slicked back with Brylcreem or other pomade.

The make of car was also an important factor in coolness: American-made muscle cars or convertibles were best—or anything with big fins. The automotive culture was big in Asheville; not only was stock car racing a favorite spectator sport, but it even provided a backdrop for movies. When a 1958 film about running moonshine, called *Thunder Road*, was filmed in Asheville, local residents got a chance to rub elbows with Hollywood personalities like the bad-boy star, Robert Mitchum. "Friends would lend their cars, or sell them, to the movie people, and Robert Mitchum would drive them," according to an interview for a West Asheville Library history project.

There were more wholesome activities too: bowling, dime-a-dance square dancing, shopping in downtown Asheville for 45 rpm records of the latest hits. The lively city already had two drive-in movie theaters on Tunnel Road, the Starlite Drive-In, with space for five hundred cars, and Dreamland Drive-In, with space for six hundred. Lawrence Welk was on television, and there was all-night gospel singing at the civic auditorium. Whew! A teenager could work up a big appetite.

Wink's, whose owners styled it "the House of Variety," had two signature attractions: the Wink Burger and the Melody Tower.

The Wink Burger, sometimes advertised as The Giant Winkburger, was a great big—four-ounce—hamburger with lettuce and tomato. "Wink's had the biggest in town, which, for teenage boys, is always the best," wrote Rick McDaniel, the food historian author of *Asheville Food: A History of High Country Cuisine*. "This is the pre-Whopper days where you either had a sack of burgers as a teenage boy, or you just got one Wink Burger and were done with it." Wink's well-rounded menu also included plenty of fried chicken and seafood selections like deep sea scallops, jumbo round shrimp and fish stick filet, all of them served with French fries, creamy coleslaw and buttered rolls.

The Melody Tower was even better. Radio station WISE had a broadcast tower at Wink's parking lot. The disc jockey, seated in his rooftop aerie, would lower a peach basket on a rope to fans below, who could write their requests and have them hoisted up. One swain was embarrassed when his request was played so quickly that he didn't have a chance to get away before the target of his secret crush could identify him.

Wink's had a few mishaps. The Melody Tower was hit by a car when a girl named Susan "was distracted by a cool '57 Chevy and the guys driving it," noted the *Asheville Citizen-Times* in 2016. The DJ was quoted as swearing, "I believe the tunnel just caved in!" Beaucatcher Tunnel, that is.

Another time, twenty-one-year-old Carolyn Yancey Kelly drove her 1958 Edsel right through a plate-glass window in front, apparently mistaking the gas pedal for the brake.

There were lawsuits, one involving a stumble over the curb late one night when the lights had been turned off and another involving a firecracker that set fire to someone's clothes. There was the obligatory grease fire.

The most intriguing incident with the law, however, involved an Episcopal minister, a teenage boy and a couple of drinks. The teenager was eventually charged with highway robbery. Newspaper coverage was specific and rather vague at the same time, a good read:

The vicar, the Reverend Albert Frost, had driven his 1959 Rambler to the Union Station bus terminal downtown one Friday to meet a friend coming in on the 10:20 p.m. bus. The friend didn't appear, but seventeen-year-old Louis Hagan, a local boy who claimed he was from Charlotte, North Carolina, was hanging around and asked the vicar for a ride to a friend's house elsewhere in town. The vicar suggested they get a drink first, so they headed to Wink's, where young Hagan had an orange soda and the vicar "a can of beer."

From Wink's, they went to Bucks, where "they ordered two beers," according to court testimony. After that, things got fuzzy. The Reverend Frost took young Hagan to meet his friend as requested, but again, no one was there. On the way back to town, it was alleged, Hagan asked Frost to stop the car for a minute. Then he attacked the clergyman, "slugged him, broke off his clerical collar and rolled him out of the automobile onto the ground."

Hagan allegedly took off with the padre's car, as well as with his engraved wristwatch, which had been a gift from "a former congregation" and was valued over $1,000, and a billfold containing $9.

Said the Reverend Frost during a preliminary hearing, "I simply wanted to be a friend to man."

Despite the challenges, Wink's was a solid business. Like Jim Buchanan of Bucks, the Winkenwerders dedicated their lives to the hospitality industry—they owned multiple motels—and succeeded in bringing modern tourism taxation and promotion practices to Asheville; the results have been a year-round rather than a seasonal destination, an international not just a regional recreation spot.

The hardworking Winkenwerder family eventually sold the drive-in to Tommy Arakas, a member of Asheville's illustrious Greek community responsible for operating many of the city's restaurants. Arakas helped introduce pizza to Asheville, and his Wink's even boasted something new called a Pizza-Burger, as well as kosher salami and corned beef. Arakas, in turn, sold Wink's to another concern, and the drive-in made way for Captain Tom's Galley.

Nowadays, Papas & Beer, a locally grown Mexican restaurant, sits where Wink's used to be.

BABE MALOY'S DRIVE-IN, SOMETIMES SHORTENED to Babe's, got underway in February 1952 at 26 Tunnel Road and within just months was garnering newspaper coverage for its popularity. "Babe Maloy's Drive-In, just beyond the tunnel on Black Mountain Highway, is one of the most attractive and popular eating spots in Asheville," gushed the *Asheville Citizen-Times*.

Its popularity is reflected in its big increases in patronage during the short time of its operation....

Parking space has been not only enlarged but the entire area has been paved, which adds to the attractiveness and cleanliness of surroundings. All equipment in the interior is new stainless steel, providing the utmost in tasty food and clean, fast service. Students from Asheville-Biltmore College serve you in your car with prompt courteous attention.

The ads for Babe Maloy's, "home of the Fat Boy," were fun.

One, with a drawing of a young boy kneeling bedside to say his prayers, sports the caption, "...and please let them take me to Babe's for Chicken in the Rough.©" That delectable, franchised new dinner was a smash hit. When it was introduced, demand outstripped supply, and Babe apologized good-naturedly to those customers who had to wait in line for their first taste. And no wonder: Chicken in the Rough, with ads showing a golf-playing rooster in mid-stroke, featured half a piping hot fried chicken with shoestring potatoes, a small jug of honey and hot buttered rolls. It was "Served at the Curb or Boxed to Go Wrapped in Aluminum Foil" and cost all of ninety-nine cents. Coffee or Coke was added for free.

People had fun at Babe Maloy's Drive-In. *Andrea Clark Photograph Collection, North Carolina Collection, Pack Memorial Public Library, Asheville, North Carolina.*

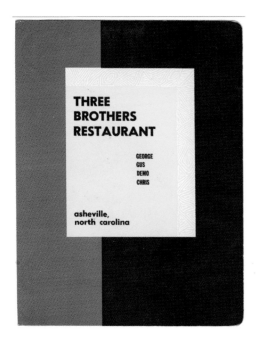

Left: Menu from Three Brothers Restaurant. *North Carolina Collection, Pack Memorial Public Library, Asheville, North Carolina.*

Below: Stone Soup's location on Broadway. *North Carolina Collection, Pack Memorial Public Library, Asheville, North Carolina.*

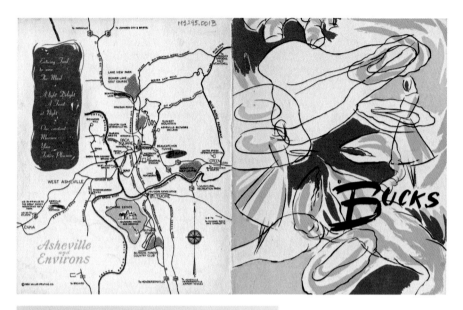

Above: Impressionistic map showing Bucks on Tunnel Road. *North Carolina Collection, Pack Memorial Public Library, Asheville, North Carolina.*

Left: Biltmore Dairy Bar cup. *From the collection of David Sparks.*

Ristorante da Vincenzo menu in an alternate spelling. *North Carolina Collection, Pack Memorial Public Library, Asheville, North Carolina.*

Matchbook from Bucks. *North Carolina Collection, Pack Memorial Public Library, Asheville, North Carolina.*

Left: Tingle's Cafe postcard. *North Carolina Collection, Pack Memorial Public Library, Asheville, North Carolina.*

Below: Swiss Kitchen exterior view. *North Carolina Collection, Pack Memorial Public Library, Asheville, North Carolina.*

Gross Restaurant, interior and exterior. *North Carolina Collection, Pack Memorial Public Library, Asheville, North Carolina.*

Swiss Kitchen dining room. *North Carolina Collection, Pack Memorial Public Library, Asheville, North Carolina.*

Biltmore Dairy Bar. *North Carolina Collection, Pack Memorial Public Library, Asheville, North Carolina.*

Dining room at Bucks. *North Carolina Collection, Pack Memorial Public Library, Asheville, North Carolina.*

Right: Merchandise display at
Swiss Kitchen. *North Carolina
Collection, Pack Memorial Public
Library, Asheville, North Carolina.*

Below: Three Brothers
Restaurant, inside and out.
*North Carolina Collection, Pack
Memorial Public Library, Asheville,
North Carolina.*

Bailey's Cafeteria and Dining Room, an immense space. *North Carolina Collection, Pack Memorial Public Library, Asheville, North Carolina.*

Rabbit's Tourist Court on McDowell Street. *Andrea Clark Photograph Collection, North Carolina Collection, Pack Memorial Public Library, Asheville, North Carolina.*

Woolworth's lunch counter, restored. *Courtesy of Erin Kellem.*

Elegant depiction of Chez Paul. *North Carolina Collection, Pack Memorial Public Library, Asheville, North Carolina.*

Above: Tastee Diner of old. *Photo by Zoe Rhine, North Carolina Collection, Pack Memorial Public Library, Asheville, North Carolina.*

Left: Ristorante da Vincenzo. *Photo by Nan K. Chase.*

Leftover signage from Silver Dollar Cafe. *Photo by Nan K. Chase.*

Tastee Diner in West Asheville. *Photo by Nan K. Chase.*

Tastee Diner lunch counter. *Photo by Nan K. Chase.*

The one-time Stone Soup. *Photo by Nan K. Chase.*

This corner was Magnolia's Raw Bar & Grille, now Brasilia Churrasco Steakhouse. *Photo by Nan K. Chase.*

The old Vincenzo's sign. *Photo by Nan K. Chase.*

Above: Timeless exterior of F.W. Woolworth Co. building. *Photo by Nan K. Chase.*

Left: Lunch counter at Woolworth Walk. *Photo by Nan K. Chase.*

From The Chef

(Cooked To Order)

Two Grilled Pork Chops with
    Applesauce 1.85
Two Breaded Veal Cutlets 1.65
Chuck Wagon Steak 1.65
Breaded Pork Cutlets 1.65
Roast Beef 1.75

T-Bone Steak	3.50
Sirloin Steak	2.95
Virginia Ham Steak	2.25

Grilled Hamburger Steak with Onions 1.45
Roast Pork 1.65
Grilled Hamburger Steak 1.35

Italian Spaghetti with Meat Sauce ... 1.35
Served with Chef's Salad and French Bread
French Fried Potatoes Not Included In This Order

Above Orders Served with Chef's Salad and French Fried Potatoes

Seafoods

(Cooked To Order)

Fried Fillet of Flounder 1.25
Fried Boneless Yellow Perch with
    Tartar Sauce and Lemon 1.45
Half Dozen Fried Oysters 1.85
Two Stuffed Deviled Crabs with
    Tartar Sauce 1.65

Combination Seafood Platter ... 1.95
Fried Flounder, Shrimp, Scallops, Crab Cake,
Lemon and Tartar Sauce

---

*Above Orders Served with Tossed Salad and French Fried
Potatoes*

Shrimp Cocktail .85

Choice of Juices .15 - .25

Half Dozen Jumbo Shrimps 1.85

Omelettes

Cheese Omelette 1.25
Western Omelette 1.35
Ham Omelette 1.25

Served with French Fried Potatoes and Toast

Cold Plates

Fresh Fruit Salad 1.00
Fresh Chicken Salad 1.00
Baked Virginia Cold Ham 1.35
Combination Cold Plate 1.65
Ham, Salami, Cheese, Hard Boiled Egg, Lettuce,
Tomato and Potato Salad

Beverages

Hot Coffee	.10	Iced Tea	.15
Hot Chocolate with Milk .	.20	Milk, ½ Pint	.15
Hot Tea	.10	Milk, Chocolate, ½ Pint	.15
Buttermilk	.15	All Soft Drinks, Small	.15
Iced Coffee	.15	Large	.25
Milk Shake	.30	Milk, Pint	.25

Fried Chicken

GOLDEN BROWN FRIED CHICKEN
One Half ... 1.65 One Fourth 1.25
Served with Golden Brown French Fried Potatoes and Salad

Above and opposite: Menu from Three Brothers Restaurant. *North Carolina Collection, Pack Memorial Public Library, Asheville, North Carolina.*

THREE BROTHERS SUPER SPECIAL

Try Our Famous

HERO SANDWICH 70
Served with Ham, Salami, Swiss Cheese, Lettuce, Tomato, Mayonnaise and Pickles

French
Fries
.30

Soups

Vegetable Soup	.30
Vegetable Beef Soup	.30
Chicken Noodle Soup	.30
Tomato Soup	.30
Clam Chowder	.30
Chili	.40

Hot Sandwiches

Hot Turkey, All White Meat	1.25
Hot Ground Steak, U. S. Choice Beef .	1.00
Hot Roast Beef	1.25
Hot Roast Pork	1.25

Above Sandwiches Served with Two Vegetables and Gravy

Tasty Salads

**Large Combination
.85**

Tossed Salad	.50
Sliced Tomatoes	.25
Cole Slaw	.25
Greek Salad, Small	.70
Greek Salad, Large	1.25

Sandwiches

THREE DECKER, Sliced Chicken, Bacon, Lettuce and Tomato, Pickle and Potato Salad	1.25
BABY CLUB, Sliced Chicken, Bacon, Lettuce and Tomato	.90

WESTERN	.70
SLICED CHICKEN SANDWICH	.70
BACON & EGG	.60
HAM & EGG	.60
COLD ROAST BEEF	.60
COLD ROAST PORK	.60
HAM & CHEESE COMBINATION	.60
GRILLED BACON & CHEESE	.60
CHUCK WAGON SANDWICH	.60
BAKED HAM SANDWICH	.60
CHIPPED HAM SANDWICH	.50
B. B. Q SLICED	.50
BACON, LETTUCE & TOMATO	.50
B. B. Q. MINCED	.45
FRESH CHICKEN SALAD SANDWICH	.40
CHEESEBURGER	.40
EGG	.30
LETTUCE & TOMATO	.30
HAMBURGER	.30
AMERICAN CHEESE	.30
AMERICAN CHEESE, Grilled	.30
HOT DOGS	.25

All the Above Sandwiches Are Served with Lettuce, Tomato, Mayonnaise and Pickles

Desserts

Strawberry Nut Sundae	.40	All Pie, Slice	.20
Chocolate Sundae	.35	Pie a la Mode	.30
Pineapple Sundae	.35	Chocolate Nut Sundae	.40
Strawberry Sundae	.35	Pineapple Nut Sundae	.40

Ice Cream (Two Dips) 20

WE SERVE — EASTLAND, TEXAS   4-67

Above: S&W Cafeteria on Patton Avenue. *Photo by Nan K. Chase.*

Left: S&W Cafeteria detail. *Photo by Nan K. Chase.*

Another sassy Babe's advertisement touted hamburgers that were "The Best in Asheville." Additional copy gave a clue to Babe's passions: "Uncle BABE Sez: 'Went fishing the other day—caught some of those BIG ones—got mighty hungry there at Fontana. Glad we took some…Chicken in the Rough along. Just as good <u>cold as hot</u>!'"

Good ol' Uncle Babe. Handsome George C. "Babe" Maloy, born in Ohio in 1916, was no stranger to risk and rewards. In World War II, he had served in dangerous conditions, both training combat pilots and as a Flying Tiger with more than three hundred missions. Maloy flew over the dreaded Burma Hump—across part of the Himalayan Mountains—and he returned home as a highly decorated veteran. He did some time as a car salesman in Ohio after the war and then moved to Asheville to strike out on his own.

Babe loved golf, fishing and the kids who circled round and round his drive-in during the relatively peaceful years after the war, and he would go on to start several other restaurants in southern cities. His fishing exploits at western North Carolina's Fontana Lake made the newspapers, and he helped run Asheville's major golf tournaments.

After Babe's death, in 2002, his son, Dennis Maloy, reminisced about his father in an *Asheville Citizen-Times* story. "He loved all those kids, and the families that would come all the way from Tennessee to eat Chicken in the Rough and rolls and honey. All the customers were like family to him, and he was so appreciative of the community for all the support they gave him. It was a magical time." (Babe's ashes were to be "scattered along Tunnel Road.")

Babe Maloy, toward the end of his life, looked back at the cruising days with tenderness: "The kids had such a good time surfing around Tunnel Road; it was good for them, gave them something to do, somewhere to be. I think all the kids had a real good time, and their parents thought it was a safe place to be, checking out the drag."

Those were the days of "parking and sparking," as youngsters courted in the last years before the advent of the birth control pill. Those were the days of imaginative but sometimes cruel pranks, like the time some boys rigged up a harness and a fake noose and were able to terrify motorists approaching Beaucatcher Tunnel by letting one of the gang dangle over the entrance, seemingly by his neck.

Those were still the days when places like Wink's would advertise only for white curb attendants and white kitchen help. The days when war-damaged veterans were sometimes ravaged by alcoholism and their high school–age children adopted the carefree escapism of the drive-in.

Those were the days that led to the Vietnam War, a conflict that fell especially hard on rural families and black inner-city kids. The coming days of race riots and burning cities, fear and distrust, the women's liberation movement, the civil rights struggle and crumbling families.

And just as American society was straining from coast to coast, something specific happened that would spell the end of Babe Maloy's, Wink's and Bucks.

According to a 2002 story in the *Asheville Citizen-Times*, the owners of the Big Three drive-ins sat down together one morning. John Winkenwerder, of the Wink's family, related, "They were having breakfast together at Bucks one morning when someone mentioned that a company called McDonald's was going to build a restaurant selling cheap hamburgers. They discussed it at length and concluded it wouldn't last a year because you couldn't make money selling 15-cent hamburgers."

By 1975, the three quirky local drive-ins were done. Fast-food franchises now ruled, thanks to their national advertising sway. They were everywhere.

CHAPTER 16

Chez Paul

On the Edge

Laissez les bons temps roulez!

Let the good times roll. And boy, did they roll at Chez Paul, an infamous roadhouse at what was then Asheville's northern boundary. An extensive seafood and steak menu with a French accent, a dance floor and live bands, late-night hours and lots of booze—those were the attractions.

The location didn't hurt. Two miles north of downtown Asheville, Chez Paul was far enough from the hubbub of daily commerce in the 1950s and 1960s for discreet dining and drinking but close enough for easy access to town. The restaurant, at 951 Merrimon Avenue, where today a suburban Ingle's grocery store operates, also had the advantage of being located on the old Dixie Highway, a pre-interstate thoroughfare linking the balmy southern states to Michigan and Ohio, in part to encourage tourism.

Chez Paul's advertisements mentioned its attractive setting near the entrance to Beaver Lake, a posh private community dating back to the 1920s. "The Garden Spot of Asheville," boasted an ad from 1951. A promotional brochure published by the Beaver Lake Park community, which was designed as a private commission by famed city planner John D. Nolen, described the lay of the land in this purple prose (leaving out the exclusionary racial covenants): "gently curving and undulating topography, almost like a succession of billowing waves, with homesites on the crests and winding streets and parkways between."

Beaver Lake, incidentally, had its own rustic history. At the turn of the twentieth century, it had been a pasture called Baird's Bottom, dotted with grazing cattle. Then, in 1919, it became Asheville's first air strip when an early aviator landed there and began commercial sightseeing tours for the grand sum of fifteen dollars each. After that, a trolley line skirted the field, connecting passengers at the end of the city line, near Grace Episcopal Church, with an excursion line to placid Weaverville to the north. After investors created the sixty-seven-acre Beaver Lake, the trolley tracks were under water.

Looking back in time, Asheville native Carole Currie, a columnist for the *Asheville Citizen-Times*, wrote about Chez Paul's reputation out there in the billowing waves of topography as she was coming of age. "My father warned me never to go there or to the Sky Club because both sold mixed drinks illegally and were regularly raided. He didn't want me caught in a raid."

Currie related that she had heard the procedure for getting an illegal drink at Chez Paul involved a waiter or waitress having to go through "a hidden door down a short hallway" to complete the order. "Conventioneers, especially, tipped well for this privilege."

Among locals, Chez Paul—or "Cheese Paul," as some folks called it—was known as a "great debauch," according to one local resident's online comments to the *Mountain Xpress* newspaper.

Chez Paul seems to have started around 1946 as Gabrielle's Famous Restaurant, featuring a "Special Chez Paul Delicious Chicken Pancake"—a crepe, perhaps—for $1.50.

By the end of 1947, the name of the restaurant had solidified as Chez Paul, and a wild New Year's Eve Bon Voyage–Farewell Dinner party that year promised a "BIG SURPRISE" just after midnight: "A brand new live baby will be given away at 12:30 A.M. January 1st, 1948…By Monsieur Charles."

Whatever that meant—possibly Monsieur Charles dressed in a diaper?

Chez Paul's management laid on the Francophile stuff pretty thick, and the lavish display ads went on and on in the most delicious ways. "We Present Our 1949 Season's Gala Opening," began an ad for that March 5 event. The wine list featured just five choices—port, sherry, Sauterne, claret and Champagne cocktail—but bore the sage advice, in French, that "*un diner sans vin, c'est comme un jour sans soleil*," which means, "A dinner without wine is like a day without sunshine."

CHEZ PAUL FAMOUS RESTAURANT
PHONE 9449 - - 951 MERRIMON AVE.,
AT THE NORTH EDGE OF ASHEVILLE
ON U. S. 19-23-25-70

A postcard showing off Chez Paul. *North Carolina Collection, Pack Memorial Public Library, Asheville, North Carolina.*

The enticing "Dinner De Famille," even if just a sop to respectability, began with a refreshing choice of chilled tomato juice, fresh fruit cocktail, Florida tangerine juice or half grapefruit and then soup du jour, fresh fruit and a relish tray. After that came an entrée from among seventeen varied choices served with Legume de Famille, Salade Francaise and dessert (along with coffee, tea or milk). The entrées included a mouthwatering array of dishes, such as half a fried spring chicken à la Maryland, Chicken Livers on Toast–Maitre d'Hotel, fried jumbo oysters Sauce Bon Vivant, baked Virginia ham Sauce Pomme, steak country style Bonne Femme, filet mignon or sirloin or T-bone broiled on charcoal and, curiously, a vegetable dinner with poached egg.

In weird contrast to this culinary lineup, the ad also included the restaurant's board of directors—perhaps a first in restaurant promotion—which included a local attorney, the clerk of city court, a swimming pool technician and "Paul Houdeille, Owner & manager." Or, as he called himself, "Monsieur Paul, Directeur."

No matter what legal troubles Chez Paul Famous Restaurant would experience over the years to come—and there were many—the menu always oozed with appeal. Spaghetti wasn't just spaghetti; it was Italian Spaghetti a la Caruse. Veal was Veal Cutlet, Milanaise. Chicken wasn't just baked or stewed; it was Fricassee a l'Indienne. The shrimp were "Shrimps à la Creole," and the filet of sole was presented with Sauce Meuniere. "Delicacies from the Sea to the Land of the Sky," the 1952 Lake Shore Dinner menu proclaimed, would include lobsters, crabs, shrimp, scallops, pompano and frog legs.

Business hours were extensive—no particular closing times were mentioned—and Chez Paul had attractive table and booth seating for one hundred indoors and more on a dining patio outside.

Police reports tell the rest of the story, or enough of it. In 1949, "beer license revoked…drunkenness and disorderly conduct in the place of business…Alleged gambling…King Bee of Gambling…Assaults.…Mr. Paul Houdeille present at bloody brawl in apartment next to restaurant…money owed…fracas."

But *le soleil* always rose brightly on the morrow. A 1949 advertisement gives a clue to the restaurant's evolution:

Now Under the Management of
Mack & Jack Fortune, who say to you
Hear Ye Folks! Hear and see!
We can't tell tales of Gay Paree.

We've never been there that is true
But CHEZ PAUL'S we know is the place for you—
To wine and dine and have some fun
The finest spot under Asheville's sun.
The service the best, the Food superb
What more can you ask? Say not a word—
Until you've give[n] us a test
Come on out, we'll do the rest.
We'll make your evening full and complete
One you'll say has been a treat.
We know what you want, we think we do
Our utmost we'll do in pleasing you.
For any occasion or any date
We'd like to help you celebrate.
Just dial the number 9-4-4-9—
And with this thought we'll end this rhyme—
Good Food, Good Wine, Good Friends, Good Cheer
That is our motto, the reason we're here:
So an invitation we extend to thee
A gay evening at CHEZ PAUL'S, OUI! OUI! OUI!

By 1952, there was new ownership ("Serving Breakfast, Lunch and Dinner"), but the more things changed, the more they stayed the same. In 1957, one of the new owners was in hot water for two counts of unlawful possession of whiskey and related charges, and that year the Alcoholic Beverage Control board revoked Chez Paul's wine and beer permit. Similar infractions continued into the 1960s.

Remember movie star Robert Mitchum? While he was in Asheville for the filming of *Thunder Road*, which apparently was shot for its 1958 release with the working title "Whippoorwill," lots of local residents had bit parts. One of them was Chez Paul waitress Sara Catonia, playing a waitress. Anyone in Asheville with dramatic aspirations had a shot at fame in "Whippoorwill," including a real police detective, an employment office manager, a television commentator, a newspaper reporter, a wrestler, a couple of country music singers, a hotel maintenance man and two Alcoholic Beverage Control agents…who played gangsters!

The '60s were the decade of big bands at Chez Paul, including such names as the Fats Diamond Combo and "poor" Bill the Singing Chef, the Kentucky Gentlemen Combo, the Gene Brown Trio, Stan the Sax Man and his combo, Fritz Albertson and His Orchestra and the Skyliners Combo. At one point, Arthur Murray dance lessons were offered there, and the restaurant continued with live music into the 1970s: Bee Bumble and the Stingers and Raw Wheat Band were two of the last.

As Asheville's suburbs reached north toward Beaver Lake and Chez Paul faded away, a rollicking bit of history came to an end.

Chapter 17

Blue Ribbon Grill

Asheville Noir

B y itself, the Blue Ribbon Grill, a predominantly African American establishment in the Eagle Street district of Asheville, could simply be seen as tragic. Frequently beset by violence, the diner exemplified a locally owned business trying to survive in a crime-ridden area.

For instance, in May 1952, Myrtle Blakely, twenty-five years old and a local resident, was shot in her right foot with a .25-caliber pistol at the Blue Ribbon Grill, and twenty-two-year-old Evelyn Frazier, an Eagle Street resident, was charged with assault with a deadly weapon. The accused woman herself took the victim to the hospital for treatment and said it was all an accident, but she was arrested there anyway and then held overnight in jail.

Later, in 1981, a man was charged with attacking his sister with a shovel at the grill.

Then, in 1986, a fight started at Blue Ribbon Grill over a two-dollar debt, and by the time the conflict moved next door to Ebony Grill and finished, one man lay dead, "shot three times in the chest with a .38 caliber handgun," according to the police report.

And in between, the Blue Ribbon Grill, at 23 Eagle Street, was broken into over and over during the 1960s and 1970s, as were numerous other businesses around town in those turbulent years; at various times, thieves took cash, food, beer and a $100 radio from the Blue Ribbon. Unlike some of Asheville's tonier mid-twentieth-century restaurants, the Blue Ribbon Grill didn't purchase fanciful display ads or arrange for upbeat press coverage; sometimes it seemed the only time the restaurant was mentioned in the newspaper was after trouble with the law.

However, such a narrow focus on individual crimes, no matter how riveting, fails to consider the larger picture of Asheville's awful economic situation in the mid-twentieth century—unique in the United States for its high level of civic indebtedness—and how the havoc wrought during the city's boom-and-bust cycle has affected residents and visitors right up to today. And a focus on individual crimes glosses over Eagle Street's prominence in downtown Asheville beginning more than two hundred years ago, just after 1800.

From a more realistic perspective, the Blue Ribbon Grill is a bit player in a larger tragedy. Take a look, then, at downtown Asheville as it skirted an urban death spiral in the years between the Great Depression and the rebirth of mass tourism in the early twenty-first century. Take a look at a layer of the city's history that has been buried beneath a recent flood tide of optimism.

"It's like a vanished landscape," observed local musician Cliff Cotton in a 2016 *Citizen-Times* interview, as Asheville's Hood Hugger tours of lost African American institutions got started.

Way back in 1901, the Asheville newspaper of the day gave a feel for the intersection of Eagle Street with South Main Street—now called Biltmore Avenue—in a story titled "Was Once a Fine Dwelling" and carrying the

Blue Ribbon Grill on a quiet Eagle Street. *Andrea Clark Photograph Collection, North Carolina Collection, Pack Memorial Public Library, Asheville, North Carolina.*

Eagle Street now redeveloped. *Photo by Nan K. Chase.*

further legends "'Greasy Corner,' Which Has Caused Police So Much Trouble for Years" and "Postoffice Was Located There and Building Was One of Best in the City." Postal service had come to Asheville a full century earlier, in 1801, when Asheville was a rough pioneer outpost but starting to grow fast. The Asheville census in 1800 listed "25 free persons and 13 slaves"; by 1900, the population was 15,000, and by 1930 it was 50,000.

The courthouse square a block to the north of Eagle Street once had stocks and a whipping post where lawbreakers might be punished publicly. Depending on the crime, a miscreant might even be branded with a hot iron right in the courtroom, a burning *M* on the palm of the hand for manslaughter, for example.

Greasy Corner was the edge of that early post office building where people wearing their tattered and greasy clothes used to rub their shoulders and unwind; the paint apparently acquired a sheen over the years. That Colonial-style building was white, with tall columns and a portico. Gradually, the structure swayed from respectability, until the town fathers discussed tearing it down. "It may not be practicable to carry it out but if it could be done it would be a great advantage in many ways, principally to the police, who find a large part of their work in that disreputable place," the story explained. "The restaurants, pool rooms and barber shops there have figured in the police court records any number of times."

The house, built most likely in the 1830s, was originally used as a private residence before becoming a store, a post office and then a restaurant. During the "military encampment" in Asheville during the Civil War, "an immense number of men" were fed there, as were the railroad laborers toiling in the 1870s to connect Asheville to the rest of the world. "The railroad hands appeared to bring more or less disorder with them as there was a good deal of drinking and that was the beginning of the corner falling into bad repute."

An "old negro woman" named Jackson ran the restaurant there. Because of her tenuous relationship with the police, she was powerless to stop the mischief. Perhaps, mused Asheville's leaders, Greasy Corner should be administered under a move-along ordinance. "The enforcement of the move-on ordinance is needed in other sections than greasy corner also. There are several places where crowds congregate and block the sidewalks, and they ought to be dispersed."

Eventually, of course, the offending building did go away, and Asheville's black business district and the residential community surrounding it grew apace.

Now, Asheville's tourist trade exploded from 1880—when rail service to the city began—until a disastrous bank crash in 1930, when most public funds on deposit were lost. Very quickly, city services dissolved as the public works department was dismissed: the streets, parks and other infrastructure began their long slide into decay, and because of huge outstanding public debt—the highest per capita in the nation—Asheville put the brakes on almost all other spending as well in order to negotiate an orderly, fifty-year repayment schedule to creditors. The high indebtedness also scared away potential investors, and so the old stock of buildings downtown rotted— no fire protection, frayed wiring and poorly functioning heaters and lax insurance coverage.

Into this morass strode Weldon Weir, a local fellow who worked his way up through the parks and recreation department, then the public works department, until he reached the position of city manager in 1950 (he was fired in 1967). Weir was an old-fashioned boss man and he got things done, as far as restarting municipal services went.

But during the 1950s and 1960s, downtown Asheville's once thriving retail district was vacating to suburban shopping malls, and soon after Weir's departure the remaining downtown businesses began seeking, and receiving, lower property tax assessments, which in turn lowered city revenue. So the city's finances continued to sink.

Urban renewal efforts slowly got underway but were heavy handed, and whole African American communities were plowed under to take advantage of federal funding. Court-ordered desegregation, which undercut the high level of black education and the black business community in Asheville, plus

Blue Ribbon Grill was located here on Eagle Street. *Photo by Nan K. Chase.*

social unrest around the Vietnam War spelled the end for Eagle diners and other storefront commerce.

The Blue Ribbon Grill's former owner, Addie J. Jones, died in 1986, leaving behind an extended family that included fourteen grandchildren, more than thirty great-grandchildren and four great-great-grandchildren.

That strip of Eagle Street is finally coming back as something new in the 2020s: a mix of upscale restaurants plus Eagle Street Marketplace, a residential and commercial project aiming to return low-cost rentals to that block.

CHAPTER 18

Stockyard Cafe

When the Farmers Came to Town

It may be hard to image nowadays, as Asheville's River Arts District grows fat with breweries, art studios and a new recreational greenway, but that low-lying part of town along the French Broad River once provided a stage for the rough-and-tumble world of livestock and farm commodities trading. The stories are legion of horse trading, horse rustling, cattle poisoning, gambling, gunplay, wild animals—and the wild characters who made it all happen. "Strange and funny things happen at the stockyards," local historian Bob Terrell once wrote.

The stockyards and auction barns, the tobacco warehouses and a freewheeling barter market existed right up until the Space Age began in the mid-twentieth century, but all of that is gone now. Instead, where the Stockyard Cafe was last located, at 157 (or 163) Craven Street, for instance, the New Belgium Brewing Company biergarten attracts an entirely different clientele.

Serving inexpensive breakfast and lunch to the farmers, the Stockyard Cafe might have existed in two different locations on opposites of the river, as did the stockyards themselves, before the little restaurant finally closed in 2004. The Western North Carolina Livestock Market itself, in its second iteration, burned in 1979.

Long, long ago, the countryside around what is now Asheville was farmland: well watered, gently rolling, mild of climate. After early American settlers pushed the Cherokee people from much of their traditional territory, they set to work clearing the land and harvesting the timber, then raising

Aerial view of the stockyards on the French Broad River. *North Carolina Collection, Pack Memorial Public Library, Asheville, North Carolina.*

cattle and swine and horses and fowl and sheep and planting hundreds of thousands of fruit trees and countless acres of tobacco and abundant crops of corn and other grains. Rich, rich farmland.

Mountain people were tough. They spun their own wool and flax and wove it into cloth for themselves; they built their own implements and wagons; and, when possible, they sold their surplus crops, even if a round trip to market on the primitive roads might take months. And while transportation improved, life still wasn't easy. One old-timer, William H. Garrett, when interviewed by the *Asheville Citizen* in 1957 at age eighty-nine, described his birthplace nearby as a two-hundred-year-old log house (putting the structure's origins, improbably, in the mid-1600s). In his younger days, the trip to town with

An intense scene at the livestock auction, near Stockyard Cafe. *Andrea Clark Photograph Collection, North Carolina Collection, Pack Memorial Public Library, Asheville, North Carolina.*

livestock for sale took two days "over Beaverdam to the sale pens." This got whittled down to just an hour with modern roads.

The Great Depression hit the region hard, and one of the ways that economic life returned was the 1931 construction of the Carolina Tobacco Warehouse on the eastern riverbank and in 1933 of the Asheville livestock market. That early livestock market specialized in beef cattle—summer pastured high in the Balsam Mountains—and sheep. There were also lively markets for horses, mules and feeder pigs.

A 1953 newspaper account of a fire that destroyed the "mule barn" on Lyman Street mentioned "a small stockyard cafe near the burning building" dating back at least to 1944 that was spared, thanks to firefighters' efforts. There is considerable confusion surrounding the correct name of the Stockyard Cafe; newspaper accounts always called it by that name, but Asheville city directories indicate that it might have been called the L&M Cafe and certainly that there were "stockyard cafes" in at least two locations along the river. Such is Asheville history: hard to nail down even in print. Let's proceed as though they are a continuing business—a part of life there.

Also in 1953, according to Asheville historian Rob Neufeld, cited in the *Asheville Citizen-Times,* the livestock operations moved to the western riverbank, and presumably the café did too. That same year, the Big Burley Warehouse,

The stockyards from above. *North Carolina Collection, Pack Memorial Public Library, Asheville, North Carolina.*

"Asheville's Newest Warehouse," opened at the Asheville stockyards on Riverside Drive; business was good, as the operators also announced they had expanded two other tobacco warehouses.

The café didn't advertise much—the health department rating was just a B—but did make news from time to time as mishaps of a criminal or simply accidental nature occurred. In 1950, for example, two very naughty thirteen-year-old boys included it in their crime wave—first slashing the fabric wings of an airplane at Carrier Field up the road, stealing more than $100 in cash from the coat pocket of a man visiting a funeral home and then breaking into the Stockyard Cafe. The boys were apprehended, as Asheville historian Rob Neufeld recounts in the *Asheville Citizen-Times*, when they spent most of the money on some flashy gun holsters and aroused suspicion (they were already on probation for having stolen bicycles). In 1959, a break-in at the Stockyard Cafe yielded $63 and a lot of cigarettes, and in 1965, the haul from a break-in included "candy, cookies, chewing gum, valued at $25." Early on, in 1949, a young bull got spooked while on a truck at the stockyards and bolted into town, where it was found the next morning in a garden but later was shot dead by police when it escaped and couldn't be caught. One time a boy stole a horse left overnight in a corral at the stockyards; ironically, the horse had been bound for the slaughterhouse as dog food.

Even more colorful than the stockyards and the livestock markets, often with hundreds of animals on the block, was the weekly barter market held on Fridays, the market auction day; some accounts have Thursday barter markets as well. Long after barter had given way to a cash economy elsewhere, fifty or one hundred cars and pickup trucks from a wide area would line the road with "wares ranging from fresh fruit to hound dogs," according to columnist Karl Fleming in the *Asheville Citizen-Times.*

The trading went like this:

Asheville is the biggest livestock market in the two Carolinas and thus provides a solid backdrop for the practice of old-times Barter as it is still carried out around here.

Farmers who come to town to sell a cow also bring, say, an old gun or a dog which they hope to sell or swap along the river....

The swapping of knives is practically an institution along the river.... The cattle market is a formal operation in the livestock yards, with buying and selling properly supervised.

But Riverside Drive in the section is also a huge pig market, but a really informal one. The farmers simply bring their pigs in aboard a pick-up truck and sell or swap them at will along the river. The animal trade also includes dogs, cats, goats, chickens, skunks, possum and even an occasional bear.

The swapping and selling of hunting dogs is carried out on a large scale, too.

There's no trace of the Stockyard Cafe on the French Broad River. *Courtesy of New Belgium Brewing Company.*

New Belgium Brewery, a recent addition to the old stockyard district. *Courtesy of New Belgium Brewing Company.*

One swap ended tragically. A sixteen-year-old boy died just hours after trading for a gun that turned out to be defective. When he and a friend, also with a gun, went to compare their weapons by laying them side by side on the ground, the faulty gun went off unexpectedly and killed the boy.

In 1979, the Western North Carolina Livestock Market then situated on the west side of the French Broad River burned down. The Stockyard Cafe remained and limped along until it closed in 2004. Where once it had fed hungry stockmen their hearty country fare, now the café's job was to reflect the rich stockyard atmosphere, a bit of the Wild West of yore. The stockyards, after all, were an institution, a chunk of cultural history. In 2005, a new regional livestock market was built west of Asheville, in Canton, to serve farmers; that was the same year that federal price supports went off tobacco. The days of farmers coming to Asheville's riverside area were over, and within a decade, there were huge changes on the ground.

The Colorado brewing enterprise called New Belgium Brewing Company purchased the eighteen-acre tract on Craven Street and has turned it into a beer production facility and a popular beer garden complex. The Stockyard Cafe is gone.

CHAPTER 19

Three Brothers Restaurant

The Proud Greeks

There were actually four brothers who ran Three Brothers Restaurant: George, Gus, Chris and Demo (short for Demosthenes) Zourzoukis. They were Greek natives, emigrating from their troubled homeland one by one starting in 1951, two years after their mother died there.

By 1956, they were all in Asheville, safe in the bosom of the city's largest immigrant community. They learned to speak English one word at a time as they slowly but surely worked their way into a comfortable middle-class existence, all the while honoring their national heritage, keeping alive the language, religion, costumes and foods of their noble Hellenic past.

When they first arrived in Asheville, the Zourzoukis brothers were still single men; only later did they start their own restaurant—and their own families—in Asheville. Still closely linked with their extended family, they took turns returning to Greece for months-long summer visits, always leaving the other three to run their restaurant, hence the name Three Brothers. During one trip, Demo had a narrow escape when he was nearly conscripted into the Greek army during sudden hostilities; even though he was over forty years old at the time, his Greek American status wouldn't have protected him, but a relative working for a Greek airline was able to help get him out safely.

Three of the brothers had been waiters, presumably in Athens, where they were reared; the fourth, Demo, was a "produce man." George came to America first, reportedly landing with a single penny in his pocket as he made his way via Ellis Island to a dishwashing job in West Virginia. Not long after that, he was asked to come to Asheville and take over a cook's spot at the Montford Cafe following the death of one of the owners. That café was located just north of downtown in the Montford neighborhood. Once he was established, he could sponsor his brothers' voyages over.

"Zourzoukis 'bought' into the partnership for $1,000 down and $50 a week," reported the *Asheville Citizen-Times* in a 1991 retrospective. "He worked hard, long hours as a cook. At that time, he said, there were about 139 restaurants in Asheville, 15 of which were owned by Greeks.

"Demo and Gus worked at the Montford Cafe, while Chris went to school. The brothers eventually bought Zourzoukis' partner's share in the business."

Business at the Montford Cafe might have continued for many years, but construction of a new bridge near that site meant condemnation, which forced a move. The brothers didn't have to go far: they relocated in a new spot at 183 Haywood Street, just south of the new bridge. Three Brothers Restaurant was born in 1959 and would operate for decades as a favorite of local residents who wanted delicious food and a place to visit with friends and catch up on news.

Three Brothers wasn't known as a Greek restaurant, necessarily, although there were hints in the menu. It was an American restaurant run by men who brought the ancient love of fine cooking with them from the old country. Their aim was "a great meal for a fair price," according to one newspaper account. And they succeeded.

The menus over the years were packed with quality. Sure, there were burgers and sandwiches. There were meaty entrées like prime rib au jus, rib eye, braised beef tips and grilled pork chops. There were salmon, flounder, rainbow mountain trout, fried crab cakes and shrimp dishes. But one densely packed menu started out with Greek flair; the generously sized appetizers included an Athenian Greek platter with feta cheese, kalamata olives and various sliced vegetables and pickles, served up with tzatziki sauce and grilled pita bread, as well as the spinach pie called spanakopita and grape leaves (dolmadakia) "stuffed with rice and marinated with lemon juice, oil, and spices." More Greek salads followed, and then came spaghetti Greek style, chicken lathoregano, lamb gyros and the house special, souvlakia, which was described as a "traditional Greek dish of pork tenderloin medallions, marinated in red wine and herbs. Served with a farmer salad and rice pilaf with gravy," all for $11.95. Greek pastries were priced at $2.00 apiece. An earlier Three Brothers menu offered less of the Greek cuisine and more mainstream American fare: hamburgers, omelets, barbecue.

Three Brothers Restaurant, now the site of Hotel Indigo. *North Carolina Collection, Pack Memorial Public Library, Asheville, North Carolina.*

More important than the restaurant as a business was the chance for the four Zourzoukis brothers to be involved in Asheville's vigorous Greek community. They and their descendants were as American as apple pie, yet they treasured their original culture and proudly nurtured its institutions: Holy Trinity Greek Orthodox Church, Greek language school for children and an annual, highly regarded Greek festival—a cornucopia of home-cooked food for anyone in town.

The local Greek community grew from about ten or fifteen families in the early 1900s to hundreds of families today, many of them originating from mountainous regions of Greece similar to the Blue Ridge Mountains surrounding Asheville. Even the mountain spirit is similar—tough and hardworking, resourceful and optimistic, family oriented and deeply religious.

The four brothers operated the restaurant together for thirty-two years, and then George Zourzoukis's son Dino bought out his share and continued the traditions for a while. In 2001, the place made way for a multimillion-dollar hotel project. As often happens, the land underneath the restaurant had become incredibly valuable, and it was time to sell.

Spanakopita

3 10-ounce packages frozen, chopped spinach, thawed
4 medium onions, chopped
6 whole green onions, chopped
¼ cup olive oil
¼ cup water
1 teaspoon salt
¼ teaspoon pepper
¼ minced fresh parsley
¼ cup minced fresh dill (optional)
1 teaspoon cream of wheat
5 eggs, beaten
1 cup cottage cheese
1½ cups crumbled feta cheese
1 pound phyllo dough
1 to 1½ cups butter, melted and warm

Drain spinach thoroughly in colander, squeezing out excess moisture. In a large skillet, sauté onions in olive oil over medium heat until tender, stirring constantly. Add spinach, water, seasoning and herbs; cook until liquid is absorbed. Sprinkle cream of wheat over top; cool.

In a large bowl, combine eggs and cheeses; stir in spinach mixture, blending well. Set aside.

Line a buttered 11-by-17-inch baking dish with phyllo dough; brush with melted butter. Add a thick layer of the spinach mixture, then top with remaining phyllo dough. Brush top layer with melted butter. Bake at 350 degrees for 55 to 60 minutes or until golden brown.
Makes 35 pieces.

Source: Three Brothers Restaurant

Kota Stifatho (Chicken Stew)

3 to 4 pounds chicken pieces
2 pounds small onions, whole
3 cloves garlic, whole
¼ cup butter

3 ounces tomato paste
1 cup chicken broth
2 tablespoons wine vinegar
Salt and pepper
1 tablespoon pickling spices
1 spiral orange peel
4 cups water or chicken broth

In a large kettle, brown chicken, onions and garlic in hot butter for 10 minutes, stirring frequently. Dissolve tomato paste in the chicken broth, add vinegar and pour over chicken. Add remaining ingredients and bring to a boil. Reduce heat, cover and simmer 2 hours or until chicken is tender and sauce has thickened. Stir occasionally. Serves 4 to 6.

Source: Asheville Greek Festival

CHAPTER 20

Bailey's Cafeteria and Dining Room

The Mall Monster Arrives

Wholesome. That was the word for the 1950s, the glorious post–World War II decade when Dad gave Mom a chaste peck on the cheek each morning as he went off to work, briefcase in hand. Mom's job was to dress attractively in a shirtwaist dress, augmented by carefully arranged hair and makeup, and to don a hostess apron and have dinner on the table at six o'clock each night. Junior and Sis were polite, helpful kids whose vocabulary relied heavily on "Gosh!" and "Swell!" Life was simple. The national economy was roaring, and the dreadful, divisive years of civil rights and anti–Vietnam War demonstrations lay beyond the horizon.

The '50s were also the years when Asheville's dynamic downtown business district, while still adding new stores and attractions, began to crumble. There would not have been a twenty-first-century rebirth of downtown Asheville if first it hadn't died. That dying took only fifteen years, but the misery lasted far longer.

Bailey's Cafeteria and Dining Room—there would be two of them built at two new Asheville malls—offered good food, warm southern hospitality, modern amenities and convenience, a nice break for the family and a good place for business and civic meetings.

The originator of Bailey's Cafeteria was William W. Bailey of Charlotte, North Carolina, but the originator of the shopping mall in Asheville was a local character named George Bryan Coggins, whose entrepreneurial spirit and pluck touched on such diverse undertakings as an anti-dandruff

The facilities at Bailey's Cafeteria and Dining Room. *North Carolina Collection, Pack Memorial Public Library, Asheville, North Carolina.*

shampoo, a vermiculite mine and, quite by accident, the city's first shopping mall. The nineteen-acre Westgate Shopping Center, which still exists, was built on a high bluff rising from the western bank of the French Broad River, just across a new Patton Avenue bridge from downtown Asheville.

What a character Coggins was! When he was only eight years old, in 1916, he was stopped by local police for driving a car into Asheville from his home in the Bee Tree Community east of town—but was let go because there was no minimum driving age then and he was doing a good job of it.

Westgate Mall was accidental because in 1955, Coggins originally planned to build an industrial plant for producing concrete and plaster on the site, which was a former rock quarry he had leased from the city and county governments as part of their bailout deal after Asheville's near bankruptcy in 1930; the contract for the concrete plant fell through when the client died, but Coggins couldn't get out of his land lease. Plan B, he realized, was to use the location, which was central by highway to nearly twenty counties thereabouts, to harness a lot of postwar buying power. Unlike downtown Asheville, the Westgate property had loads of free parking, and private car ownership was exploding; in one three-month period in 1958 the city bus system lost a quarter of its ridership.

Since there were no other shopping malls in North Carolina at the time, Coggins studied facilities out of state before drawing up plans, soliciting tenants and arranging financing. Westgate opened in 1956, and Bailey's Cafeteria opened there the following year, one of thirty retailers clustered under sheltered walkways.

William Bailey had started out as a baker's apprentice, and by the time he opened his cafeteria at Westgate, he had already started and sold a cafeteria in Myrtle Beach, South Carolina, and started another cafeteria in Charlotte. Eventually, his company ran a chain of at least eight cafeterias stretching across Virginia and both Carolinas. Bailey boasted in 1966 that his restaurants had served three million meals in the previous year.

He had always enjoyed cooking and was actively involved in menu development and kitchen operations. In an unusual move, William Bailey liked to make his recipes available to the public.

"I still like to go back and put on my apron when I see things out of line," he told the *Asheville Citizen-Times* as a successful chief executive. His menu favorites included "Maryland baked chicken, buttermilk custard pie and egg custard pie," in addition to roast beef, char-broiled steak, country fried steak and plain fried chicken, plus irresistible strawberry shortcake.

The gigantic Bailey's in the Westgate Shopping Center was so much fun, with rows and rows of square four-seat tables lined up on shiny linoleum, long steam tables and dramatic up-lighting toward the tray ceiling.

Those were the days of imaginative promotions aimed at getting Mom and the rest of the family into the mall and shopping. After all, the parking lot held 1,200 cars.

One Westgate advertisement in 1958 touted $200 "In Valuable Prizes" for the lucky winner of a Mother of the Year contest. The winner would be announced at a brief Mother's Day party at Bailey's beginning at ten o'clock in the morning, with free coffee and donuts for all the moms. The loot consisted of this improbable mix:

1 Pair of Ladies' Summer Shoes
Croquet Set
Dinner for Six
Dinner for Two
Plastic Hamper
Plastic Swimming Pool
$25 Gift Certificate
Portrait of Winner Complete with Frame

1 Qt. Super Kem-Tone
1 Qt. Kem-Glow Enamel
1 Year Supply Printed Checks
Whitman's Sampler
Ladies' Handbag
5 Gallons Gasoline
Electric Pop-Up Toaster
Beautiful Spring Dress
Two Free Shoe Repairs
Jeweled Wastebasket and Matching Kleenex Dispenser
1 Cured Ham
$25 Mdse. Coupon Book
2 Bags of Shredded Foam Rubber

To win Mother of the Year, hopeful contestants had only to fill out one or more coupons—no limit on the number—at any Westgate store.

A later Westgate Shopping Center promotion, this one for the spring and summer fashion show, gave away a side of beef—cut and wrapped courtesy of Winn-Dixie supermarket. Just register at any participating store to win.

Bailey's Cafeteria offered lots of space for meetings. *North Carolina Collection, Pack Memorial Public Library, Asheville, North Carolina.*

The Westgate Bailey's was open for lunch and dinner six days a week, closed Sundays. Soon enough, in July 1966, there was a second Bailey's Cafeteria in Asheville, the largest in the Bailey's chain. This one was located in the new Tunnel Road Shopping Center & Mall, later reborn as Innsbruck Mall—not to be confused with the Asheville Mall, also on Tunnel Road, which would open in 1973.

This second cafeteria was open every day, but all the menu items were the same at the two outlets. There was so much to eat: ten meat entrées, eight vegetable selections, sixteen salads, half a dozen different breads, fried oysters on Friday nights and all those cakes, pies and puddings. As William Bailey boasted, "The Two Best Places to Eat…Home and Bailey's."

But food was only half the picture. Bailey's Cafeterias hosted every kind of meeting under the sun, from an engineers' association to the Asheville Jaycettes. The ambience was just right for modern socializing: big rooms, a lot of helpful staff, variety and optimism.

Malls came to Asheville more than half a century ago, and now styles of shopping have changed drastically. Shopping centers all over the United States are folding or at least rethinking the mix. And just as all fashions change, the mall cafeteria has run its course. For now.

CHAPTER 21

Biltmore Dairy Bar

Pride of Asheville

Fat, fat, fat and more fat.

The Biltmore Dairy was all about fat—butterfat—and by extension the Biltmore Dairy Bar was all about fat too. People loved it! Luscious lickable ice cream cones, towering sundaes and thick milkshakes in pastel hues, and they all began with Biltmore Dairy's high-butterfat milk—16 to 18 percent—which was processed at a new bottling plant next door. It was a "temple of butterfat," wrote one admiring newspaper reporter.

Famous indeed was the original Winky Bar, consisting of "vanilla ice cream with maraschino cherries and peanuts, all dipped in chocolate and stuck on a stick," according to a look back by Asheville journalist Jason Sandford in 2010. A reprise of that dish was being offered at Biltmore Estate's then-new Creamery at Antler Hill Village; it was called the Winky Bar Sundae, featuring "black cherry ice cream on waffle cone topped with whipped cream and a cherry."

One super-sundae featured at the now defunct Biltmore Dairy Bar, referred to good-naturedly in promotions as the Pig's Dinner or the Pig's Trough, reportedly consisted of more than twenty scoops of ice cream, suitable for a group of teenagers out for a good time. It happened.

From about 1956 or 1957, when Biltmore Dairy Bar opened at the prestigious address of 1 Vanderbilt Road, until the late 1990s or early 2000s, when it finally became too cumbersome for the Vanderbilt heirs to operate, that restaurant on the southern edge of Biltmore Village delighted generations of Asheville locals. It was sorely missed when it closed. Today, the site of the

Drive in. There is room for 200 guest cars. Customers may eat at the Dairy Bar or attend a meeting in the John Cecil Room, provided for civic and club functions by Biltmore Dairy Farms in the new building. This entrance is from Hendersonville Road.

Biltmore Dairy Bar on today's Hendersonville Road. *North Carolina Collection, Pack Memorial Public Library, Asheville, North Carolina.*

bottling plant and dairy bar is occupied by the five-story DoubleTree by Hilton Asheville-Biltmore hotel and a TGI Friday's restaurant.

The Biltmore Dairy Bar on what is now called Hendersonville Road was the flagship location of a chain of Biltmore Dairy processing plants that eventually spread over five southern states, many of them with a popular dairy bar next door to help siphon off the incredible excess of, well, fat.

The world has George Vanderbilt to thank.

George Washington Vanderbilt is known far and wide today as the creator of the Biltmore Estate in Asheville, its fairy tale mansion and spectacular gardens. Together, those core operations of the original estate attract well over one million visitors a year from around the world.

Less well known is George Vanderbilt's dominant role in establishing large-scale farming on some of the 125,000 acres he once owned there. Vanderbilt's mansion was completed in 1895, and after his widowed mother died in New York in 1896, the son was free to devote ever more energy to realizing his *beau idéal*: a modern, progressive farm system grounded in scientific management, not tradition. Eventually, the baronial-size Biltmore Estate produced Berkshire hogs, as well as sheep and poultry, plus fruits and vegetables, even bees for honey and sorghum for molasses; some 1,200 acres alone were devoted to raising high-yield grain crops for the animals. Manure went back into the ground to keep it as productive as possible. Vanderbilt was a true "locavore," desiring that as much food as possible that was consumed on the estate be raised there as well.

In the process of building his livestock operations, Vanderbilt restored to health great swaths of logged-over mountainsides and eroded fields. The proof of his passion was in the dairy operations, his most successful endeavor from a market standpoint and, for a long time after his untimely death in 1914, his most enduring contribution to the Asheville community. Vanderbilt didn't live to see the far-flung effects of his stewardship, but he was recognized with gratitude right from the start.

"It is Vanderbilt the farmer, not Vanderbilt of the Chateau, who has proven to be the great benefactor of Western North Carolina," stated the *Asheville News and Hotel Reporter* in an 1897 number.

> *Today he is the best farmer in the South....*
>
> *Anyone who knew the barren hills, the washed out gullies, sedgefields, swamps, ditches, and the succession of worn out farms and their tumbledown houses—in which their owners were starving—that a short while ago occupied the site of the new splendid and fertile Biltmore Estate is struck with amazement at the marvelous change that has been wrought by the wise expenditure of money on the most desirable and beautiful location in the world.*

Hundreds of farm families were settled around the estate to do the daily work. There were so many estate farmers' families that they had their own country fair each fall; Edith Vanderbilt, George Vanderbilt's down-to-earth and popular wife—nicknamed Lady Vanderbilt by the help—would make an appearance and sometimes even drive a tractor.

Vanderbilt started building his famed dairy herd with one hundred Jersey cows, likely purchased from West Asheville's own Edwin Carrier, who built much of that town's infrastructure and was also a stockbreeder. From there, Vanderbilt expanded his dairy herd to some two thousand head, with perhaps twenty sires, making purchases wherever the pedigrees led, even overseas. The yields of milk broke records and won prizes, as described in Biltmore Farms archives:

> *For many years the Biltmore Farms Jersey herd was "on show" in many parts of the country. They were successful in winning prizes in the leading*

cattle shows both in the United States and, from time to time, in Canada. Specially outfitted freight cars carrying the herdsmen, the cattle, and feed and supplies would leave Asheville in mid-August and return around Thanksgiving. During this time they would exhibit at shows all over the East, South, and Midwest. In 1952, Biltmore animals were the Grand Champion Bull and Grand Champion Cow in the National Jersey Show. The fact that these animals were bred, owned, and exhibited by the same farm established a record that remains unbeaten to this day.

A cow named Financial Madam Bess, milked four times a day at her prime, "produced more than 21,000 pounds of milk in 10 months," according to a 2014 profile of the dairy in *Our State* magazine.

The original estate dairy building, still on the Biltmore Estate but now a winery, was state-of-the-art when completed in the late 1800s, with central heating for the cows, pipelines cooled with ice to carry milk hygienically from the barn, automated underground waste removal and on and on. It took up a total of nearly 100,000 square feet. One result was happy cows and so much milk that local hospitals got it for free, and soon a dairy bar opened next door to the barn, open to the public, to help manage the overflow of product.

A more important outcome was the rapid establishment of Biltmore Dairy as *the* commercial dairy first in Asheville and then in all surrounding communities—and surrounding states. Vanderbilt's dairy had a resident veterinarian and a bacteriologist, and the dairy products soon became known for their freshness and purity. Because Biltmore Dairy had the only large-scale pasteurization facility in the South at that time, it also bought milk from outside farmers for processing and distribution. The business was a cash cow, so to speak.

There was almost no limit to the products that Biltmore Dairy delivered to local homes and businesses: vitamin D whole milk, cream and buttermilk; regular cheese, cottage cheese and butter; chocolate-, strawberry- and orange-flavored dairy drinks; and ice cream galore. Oddly, no one drank skim milk in those days, as it was considered fit only to feed to hogs.

In the early years, horse-drawn Biltmore Dairy delivery wagons were a familiar sight around town, later updated to a fleet of modern panel trucks painted with "really rich, orangey yellow and black" stripes and manned by an army of drivers in "crisp white uniforms and bow ties," according to *Our State* magazine.

One of the favorite Biltmore Dairy products, which was served at the Dairy Bar and sold elsewhere, was molded and decorated ice cream, including shapes from flowers to animals to famous personalities to holiday-themed motifs. The process was complicated, as Biltmore Farms historical documents show:

> *It was a very time consuming and labor intensive process. From a tub of already frozen ice cream a mold would be filled and then sent back to the hardening room to allow the ice cream to take the shape of the mold. Next day the mold would be brought back out, quickly dipped in hot water to loosen the contents, which were then placed on dry ice. The ice cream would then be decorated, placed on a tray, and returned to the freezer room. Subsequently the finished product would be brought out again, wrapped, and packed in a cardboard box with dry ice for delivery to the customer's home.*

As luck has it, visitors to Asheville today can see some of the elaborate hinged ice cream molds in a display case in the lobby of the DoubleTree hotel on the old dairy bar site. One of the Biltmore heirs, now deceased, kept hundreds more of the leftover molds.

By the 1950s, with expansion throughout the South, even Biltmore Dairy's local processing needs outgrew the estate proper. Thus, the new bottling plant and restaurant served breakfast, lunch and dinner in addition to the desserts. With its clean, modern styling and spacious interior, Biltmore Dairy Bar was an instant hit. The sign outside said it all: "Supreme in Quality."

Thirty years after the dairy bar opened, the economics of milk retailing had changed: supermarkets took over from home delivery, and the profits from hotel development began to look very good instead. The Biltmore Company pulled back its regional reach and then separated the dairy business from the parent company and finally sold the division to Pet Inc. in 1985.

Biltmore Dairy Bar on Hendersonville Road stayed open a while longer as a stand-alone business a block from the estate entrance. There was a major face-lift reported both in 1989 and 1999, but within a few more years, the family had decided not to stand in the way of national branding and consumer trends, and the dairy bar closed.

CHAPTER 22

Bavarian Cellar

The Longest Happy Hour, the Weirdest Mall

Even in its heyday, Asheville's Innsbruck Mall looked about as much like an Alpine village as a rusted-out pickup truck looks like a new Cadillac. No comparison, but nice try!

Tunnel Road, on Asheville's near east side, continued to develop in the 1960s and the 1970s in a dual role: as a zone for tourists to book motel rooms and dine conveniently, and as a regional shopping magnet as malls were built. After the pioneering Westgate Shopping Center, which opened in West Asheville in 1956, a small shopping center went into south Asheville in 1963, and then in 1966 came the completion of the Tunnel Road Shopping Center. Bavarian Cellar was an early tenant.

"Too big for one photograph," ran the caption on a newspaper photograph of the newest mall: twenty acres, more than 1,600 parking spaces, almost a quarter million square feet of retail space, dozens of stores and two levels, almost unheard of at the time. Various accounts of its construction stress it was "carved" from one flank of Beaucatcher Mountain, and indeed some 300,000 cubic yards of earth were removed for grading.

Within twelve years, the Tunnel Road Shopping Center was undergoing what the *Asheville Citizen-Times* described as "extensive renovations" to the interior, and it would be reborn, in 1976, as Innsbruck Mall, "a Bavarian village…that will resemble the Austrian city of Innsbruck."

The mall will offer a completely Bavarian look, with the Bavarian Cellar restaurant representing the ultimate goal for the overall atmosphere.

Other features will include large wooden beams, low shingled roofs, custom designed windows, a landscape of plants and red flowers, and the famous "Golden Roof," native to Main Street in Innsbruck.

Innsbruck Mall, then, may have been the first themed shopping mall in the nation and certainly the first to latch onto Bavarian style.

The early facelift was considered crucial to rejuvenating customer traffic. The soon-to-be-renamed Tunnel Road Shopping Center was unusual in having no major national department store as a retail anchor. Rather, it had a mix of local and regional stores, and while quirky and attractive to Asheville residents, this proved a less than ideal business model. The hours were short too: open until 6:30 p.m. weekdays and closed Sundays.

The Charlotte-based mall owners decided that publicity was the answer to their woes and approached the gingerbread makeover as a way to get press coverage and, thus, customer interest. They hired Charlotte architect Friedrich H. Schmitt—German by birth—and he chose the theme.

"When I first came to Asheville to look at the center, I noticed the city was surrounded by mountains," Schmitt told the *Asheville Citizen*. "After taking under consideration the climate and the tourists, everything just resembled Innsbruck."

Unlike the original Innsbruck, though, the rebranded mall would have "a landscaped television area for children," among other amenities. Schmitt told the reporter, "We want a completely village-type atmosphere, not a commercial one." An October 1 Octoberfest Sale was the kickoff event.

The place was bizarre through and through—an early ad presciently boasted, "It's like shopping in another world"—and during most of the next forty years, vast stretches of the storefronts would remain empty. But Innsbruck Mall clung to life until nearly 2020.

Students of American mall history have compiled a lot of lore about Innsbruck Mall on the Sky City Retail History blog. Certain words and phrases jump out from the many pages of reminisces about the place: "always high on vacancies…a little deserted…mold issues…inappropriate windows…green Astroturf…plants growing wildly…dead…burnt out light bulbs…mystery spaces…a really fluky place." A double stairway between levels was flanked by a pair of rare slim-line escalators. For much of the mall's existence, a North Carolina Division of Motor Vehicles office was all that brought people inside the complex; otherwise, photos of the interior are devoid of humans. Outside, panhandlers harassed customers going to their cars.

As for Bavarian Cellar, imagine the setting: the restaurant was tucked away in the lower part of the mall around back, and the atmosphere was dark and "datey" in a grown-up way that local youths found irresistible, perhaps because of the casual way management enforced the age limit for drinking. The advent of mixed drinks in Asheville in 1979, after nearly seventy-five supposedly "dry" years, boosted business and added a sheen of sophistication to places like the Bavarian Cellar. Before that, there was just beer and wine service, but that was enough to make the bar a hangout for regulars.

One admiring Asheville native, posting anonymously on the Sky City Retail History website, wrote, "It had a great bar and when you went down there it was like walking into a beer hall in Munich." *Really* like Munich. This same blog participant added that "once Hitler's Mercedes-Benz (it was gold color) was on display in the open area of the second level."

The food at Bavarian Cellar was described simply as "great." It was rich and hearty, flavorful and slightly exotic. One local recalled a lasting memory of veal with black cherry sauce. The early menu concentrated on homemade German soups and dinners, "continental sandwiches" and more

Bavarian Cellar was tucked away behind Innsbruck Mall. *North Carolina Collection, Pack Memorial Public Library, Asheville, North Carolina.*

than thirty kinds of beer and wine, both domestic and imported. A private dining room called the Sabre Room was available, and patrons could use what was relatively new in 1968: a charge card.

A later menu—after a change in management in 1980—had expanded to include classic German entrées, Bavarian Deutsche sausage plates and a Bavarian sausage platter for two, char-broiled specialties and sandwiches, Italian favorites, seafood and rich "Continental Desserts."

> *Everything's NEW*
> *At The Old Bavarian Cellar!*
> *NEW Management! NEW Menu! NEW Chef!*
> NEW Boar's Head Lounge! NEW Happy Hour, 4 P.M.–TIL!
> NEW Sunday Hours!

There was good reason for new management. The old management couldn't seem to stay out of trouble. In 1971, a former chef at Bavarian Cellar, Charles Cohelia, pleaded guilty and turned state's evidence in the trial of four other men, but he still got a ten-year prison term; together, the five had stolen a safe from the restaurant. According to the *Asheville Citizen-Times*, "Cohelia described how the theft was planned, difficulties encountered in loading it [the safe] in an automobile after removing it from the Cellar, and, finally, the opening of the safe with a sledgehammer and a crow bar in a wooded section near Asheville Airport." The take was $300.

Four years later, Joseph Franklin Link, the "former proprietor" of the Bavarian Cellar and a companion restaurant at the mall that shared a kitchen with it, Giuseppe's Restaurant, was charged with multiple counts of receiving stolen property following a series of break-ins around Asheville. The stolen property included hundreds of turquoise rings and a great deal of other Indian jewelry. Oddly, the same Link had, in 1969, placed a classified ad for some high-end commercial-grade cooking equipment, "used only three months." He even listed Bavarian Cellar as the place to contact him.

In 1976, the Bavarian Cellar lost $3,000 of food and equipment during an audacious early morning break-in. Inside job? The *Citizen-Times* provided detail: "Carol J. Link, the proprietor…said the items stolen included four kegs of beer, 40 pounds of hamburger, nine gallons of milk, two cases of mushrooms, two cases of high-ball glasses, two cases of tea glasses, two cases of beer mugs, a case of beer pitchers, a large quantity of bread and an assortment of steaks, hams and cheeses." This was obviously before the days of security cameras monitoring every door.

And in 1978, the Coca-Cola Company got into the act, suing Bavarian Cellar (Joseph F. Link, manager) over allegations that waitresses had offered diners Coca-Cola but served something else, namely, Pepsi, the only cola available there. Coke executives had issued three prior warnings against the practice before finally suing, according to a newspaper account.

Despite all the travails, the Bavarian Cellar continued to offer a comfortable, clubby appeal and so much fattening food. Sometime after a final 1982 holiday "Deutsche blast" featuring a giant buffet of "all the wursts any German could think of, packaged by Ussingers, one of the best German meat packers in the U.S.A.," the Bavarian Cellar faded away.

There's a postscript. After that restaurant vacated the mall, a popular new downtown restaurant with Indian roots, The Windmill European Grill, was outgrowing its space and opened a spinoff at the old Bavarian Cellar site. The Windmill European Grill/Il Pescatore offered a marvelous German-Italian-Asian fusion. "You could get a jagerschnitzel and a damn curry at the same place," marveled the future celebrity chef Vijay Shastri. More of him in a later chapter.

Today, Innsbruck Mall, at 85 Tunnel Road, may be slated for total redevelopment in a modern mixed-use plan. The owners have remained tight-lipped among swirling rumors.

CHAPTER 23

High Tea Café

Resurrection

Before there was Starbucks—just barely—there was High Tea Café, the place to savor a lovingly brewed beverage and a warm muffin and talk among friends.

High Tea Café was the sweetest place. But it had an edge. It had to.

Started in 1974 and lasting only until 1983, the combination tea shop, art gallery and performance space was nonetheless an important new business and cultural driver in the resurrection of downtown Asheville. More than that, High Tea set the tone of fresh, imaginative cuisine that would mature over the next few decades and put Asheville on the path toward culinary fame.

You could say that High Tea Café was the love child of naïveté and hope, fed by desperation.

When the little café at 23 Wall Street got started, there was almost no night life in downtown Asheville. That's because people were afraid to be there after dark. Unlikely as it seems today, downtown Asheville was referred to as a ghost town: seedy, with beer joints, prostitution and an X-rated theater and peep shows.

Back in the mid-1970s, the downtown had been hollowed out after shopping malls took hold, and in fact, over a decade or so the city's population fell by 10 percent.

There was a "general air of despair" among people trying to start businesses in that area, admitted Chandler "Chan" Gordon, "but there is change in the air." Chan and his wife, Miegan, were to open the iconic

Miegan Gordon, *seated*, and Nancy Orban at High Tea Café. *North Carolina Collection, Pack Memorial Public Library, Asheville, North Carolina.*

bookstore The Captain's Bookshelf around the corner from High Tea Café in 1976. Their business was one of the success stories and operated for more than forty years.

The first hopeful signs of renewal were showing up as the city government and entrepreneurs in the private sector learned how to work together for the common goal of commercial success and expansion of the tax base, creating partnerships that would move the civic ship out of the doldrums.

A big factor in this push was a close call with urban renewal disaster: the real possibility that developers would tear down eighty-five distressed buildings over seventeen acres—eleven city blocks—centered on today's lively, eclectic North Lexington Avenue, and replace them with a giant multipurpose mall that would include department stores, hotels and convention facilities. Amid bitter political strife, voters went to the polls and defeated funding for the project; after that, the rising tide of smaller-scale historic restoration began.

Wall Street, at that time a quiet, tumble-down alley just north of Patton Avenue and south of Battery Park Avenue, was home to a surprising number of shops despite its rough condition. Among almost four dozen listed in a cookbook compiled by Nancy Orban, a founder of High Tea

Café, were Waechter's Silk Shop, Wick & Greene Jewelers, Asheville Reweaving Service, Wall Street Music Shop, Humpty Dumpty Shoe Shop and Gloria's Bride Shop.

"When I first started, downtown was deader than a doornail," Orban told the *Mountain Xpress* newspaper for a history of Asheville's food culture. "Rent was only $60, so you could really try anything. And it seemed safe to open up a restaurant."

The little café initially opened with long weekend hours—until midnight Thursday through Saturday. "Those evening hours were soon dropped because of lack of customers," Orban wrote in the foreword to *The High Tea Café No Frills Recipe Book*, which she compiled in 1977 and republished in 2001. "Instead, we opened earlier and served simple breakfasts: scrambled eggs with an individual loaf of French bread (made especially for us by a local baker), soft-boiled egg with an English muffin, and the Ralph Burns (cheddar cheese, a hard-boiled egg, wheat toast, and coffee)."

The warm, welcoming atmosphere of the café was so attractive, according to Orban, that some early customers came in with their own sausage biscuits and then ordered beer and left a mess behind. That's when the No Sandwiches sign went up.

Nancy Orban, a founder of High Tea Café. *North Carolina Collection, Pack Memorial Public Library, Asheville, North Carolina.*

Inside the cozy High Tea Café on Wall Street. *North Carolina Collection, Pack Memorial Public Library, Asheville, North Carolina.*

High Tea Café was part business, part cooperative, with lots of people pitching in to do chores. Oban and her partner, Molly Lay, both having moved to Asheville from San Francisco, took turns cooking. The menu quickly expanded to include more than one hundred selections in various combinations. A hefty majority of the revolving menu comprised soups, for the "soup-crazy" diners who would order any soup they could.

At High Tea, that meant starting with a good stock, either vegetable or chicken. Because the café didn't really have a kitchen, the soups had to be assembled from ready-made components and then warmed to serving temperature. Frozen vegetables played their part, as did canned stock when homemade wasn't available.

Desserts actually took top billing on the High Tea menu board because sweet treats are wonderful with a glass of steaming tea, cocoa or spiced coffee. There were a few entrées, then salads made with whatever came to hand and tossed with freshly made dressings. No coffee was served older than twenty-five minutes after brewing ("There is no justification for serving it," Orban wrote).

Her amazing cookbook, long out of print, spelled out the priorities: of the more than 140 recipes, 51 were for soups, everything from a yummy Potato-

Presenting High Tea Café on Wall Street. *North Carolina Collection, Pack Memorial Public Library, Asheville, North Carolina.*

Bill of fare at High Tea Café. *North Carolina Collection, Pack Memorial Public Library, Asheville, North Carolina.*

Swiss Cheese soup to Senegalese Chicken; the only soup recipe that never caught on, apparently, was a cold beet borsch.

Salads bore the names of favorite customers (there were thirty-seven salads listed, including Battery Park Salad and Cumberland Circle Salad, after local landmarks, plus eight dressings). When it came to entrées, the Quiche Penland was a favorite.

Graphic arts and performance art had a home at the High Tea Café, including the Blue Plate Special theatre troupe, photo exhibits and lots of music.

The Bill of Fare for High Tea Café listed the light desserts first—from cinnamon toast for fifty cents to a Mocha Velvet sundae for a dollar— because that's what people really needed. Under the heading "Coffees," the Café Borgia consisted of "chocolate coffee with whipped cream and orange peel shavings. 65 cents."

In the end—1983—High Tea and a lot of the other early Wall Street businesses moved elsewhere or closed when a major urban renewal initiative redid Wall Street with improved infrastructure and rents went up.

BECAUSE HIGH TEA CAFÉ DID not have a full kitchen, all recipes were adapted to use canned or frozen components when possible for ease of assembly and heating. The following recipes are from the *High Tea Café No Frills Recipe Book*

Apple-Butterscotch Cake (Jinny Hamilton)

2 c. sugar
1 c. vegetable oil
3 lg. eggs
3 c. pared and diced apples
1½ c. flour
1 t. cinnamon
1 t. salt
1½ c. broken nuts (your choice)
1 t. soda
1 t. baking powder
6 oz. butterscotch chips

Preheat oven to 350°.

Combine sugar, oil, eggs and hand mix. Mix in apples, then all other ingredients except butterscotch. Pour into a 10 by 12 pan. Spread chips on top. Lower temperature to 325° and bake for 50–55 minutes.

Velvet Broccoli Soup

10-oz. package frozen broccoli flowerets
3 c. chicken or vegetable stock
1 bay leaf
1 med. onion, chopped
1 T. butter
1 c. whole milk
Salt and ground white pepper to taste
4 lemon slices, thin

Add chicken stock, broccoli, onions, and bay leaf to a stock pot. Bring to a boil, reduce heat, cover, and simmer 6–7 minutes, until broccoli is tender. Discard bay leaf. Put half of soup through a blender until quite smooth. Return to soup, reheat, and add butter. Stir in milk and add salt and pepper. Float a lemon slice on each serving.

Miegan Salad

Leaf lettuce
¼ watermelon, balled
1 cantaloupe, balled
2 bananas, sliced
Miegan dressing
½ pint of blueberries
Pecan pieces

Arrange the melons on a bed of lettuce and scatter the bananas. Dress, then garnish with berries and pecans.

Miegan Dressing

1 c. mayonnaise
4 oz. whipping cream
2 T. red currant jelly

Mix together in a blender and refrigerate. Use the day you make it.

Eggnog Colbert

Mix together 1 ½ c. of whole milk and 2 egg yolks. Add 1 c. of vanilla ice cream and mix until creamy. Add ¼ t. each of cinnamon and nutmeg, and 4 oz. white rum. Beat together until smooth and serve in small wine glasses.

Orange Marie
(Must make three days ahead.)

6 T. malted milk powder
6 oz. thawed frozen orange juice
18 oz. water (use juice can)
18 oz. ginger ale

Combine ingredients in a glass jar with a tight cap. Shake well and refrigerate for three days. Shake before serving.

CHAPTER 24

Stone Soup

Bread, Soup and People Power

D o you recall the fairy tale called "Stone Soup"? In that delightful old-world story, hungry soldiers approach a town where the inhabitants have hidden all their food for safekeeping. In a mild form of trickery, the soldiers decide they will teach the townspeople to make stone soup.

First, they tell the townspeople they need a big pot of boiling water. Easily done. Then they add the basic component, stones, and perhaps a bit more: some meat, a few carrots and a cabbage, salt and pepper, barley and milk. Little by little, the townspeople bring the ingredients out from hiding places, and before long, there's a steaming cauldron of delicious soup. They bring tables and benches, and without anyone's being threatened, they learn they can share a feast and lose their fears. It's a heartwarming lesson about cooperation and contentment. About human progress.

That was Asheville's Stone Soup, which opened in 1977, did business in four different locations and finally departed the scene in 1994. *Asheville Citizen-Times* writer Barbara Blake said Stone Soup "helped usher in the city's slow-food movement and launched a generation of forward-thinking movers and shakers whose passion for social justice continues today."

Not just a soup-and-sandwich shop, Stone Soup evolved as a pioneer of Asheville's farm-to-table movement. The in-house bakery quickly expanded beyond the dining room to supply restaurants and grocery stores in North Carolina and beyond and may have been the first business in the area to

Stone Soup called this former gas station home for a while. *North Carolina Collection, Pack Memorial Public Library, Asheville, North Carolina.*

grow alfalfa sprouts. Stone Soup also did some sharecropping, growing or harvesting fruit and vegetables to use in the kitchen.

"Broccoli for many bowls of Swiss broccoli chowder were grown, harvested, blanched and frozen during those two [early] years—lots of strawberry shortcake, too," explained founder Dick Gilbert much later to the *Asheville Citizen-Times*. "And that's where we first started growing sprouts for use in the restaurant and for sale at local supermarkets—we were the first into the market with those, and we continued that program until the big boys with a huge equipment advantage took over the sprouts market."

Stone Soup helped launch Asheville's big, diverse music and performance scene, providing a stage for groups ranging from an amateur Shakespeare company to an expert on the art of dowsing to folk singers and blues artists.

Stone Soup was an early employee-owned enterprise, "one of the oldest worker-owned businesses in the state," according to the *Asheville Citizen-Times*. One version of the story, reproduced on the menu, put it this way:

> *Stone Soup began in 1977 as a fund raising project for a United Methodist social service project. The group responsible for the program*

eventually decided that "doing business" was more important than their service program. They set out to create businesses that would be owned by their workers, fair to their customers and that would offer useful, worthwhile goods and services. Today, Stone Soup is an established retail and wholesale bakery, two restaurants, caterer, weekend night spot and a successful model of a worker-owned, group-led organization. All food is prepared "from scratch" from Stone Stoup's famous baked breads & pastries to their soups!

A 1985 business profile in the *Carolina Sun* titled "Stone Soup Operates with Novel Employee-Owner System" explained the model with wonderment:

The business is run by worker-owners. Anyone who works 10 hours or more becomes a partial owner in the business. "We are all equal owners no matter how much we work," said Gilbert. From dishwasher to coordinator, their salaries are also equal.

"We make all our own decisions by consensus. There is no majority rule, everyone has to agree....

"Whether somebody becomes a worker-owner or not, everyone has to agree and if they don't the person doesn't get to be a worker-owner. Not only that, they don't even to keep their job. That's really a tough deal," said Gilbert.

In keeping with egalitarian spirit, tipping was not allowed.

Stone Soup got its start at the Allen Center, which in turn was housed at the old Allen School, a private high school for African American girls on Asheville's College Street that operated from 1887 to 1974. Dick (a "bearded, twinkly-eyed father figure," according to one description) and Mary Gilbert ("the quiet soldier who oversaw the kitchen operations and was everyone's mom") were deeply committed to social justice causes and had been asked to help create community programs with a jobs component. Thus began Stone Soup in an upstairs cafeteria in 1977.

Three years later, Stone Soup moved to the historic Manor Inn on Charlotte Street. The Manor Inn, which opened in 1899, was a glorious pile of decorative woodwork and brick, but it was in an advanced state of decay by 1980. Nonetheless, Stone Soup stayed there until the so-called Great Super Bowl Blizzard of 1984, "when the building essentially froze to death and was condemned by the city six weeks later—subsequently bought and restored to grandeur by the Preservation Society."

The staff of worker-owned Stone Soup. *North Carolina Collection, Pack Memorial Public Library, Asheville, North Carolina.*

Meanwhile, the café moved to a new home at 50 Broadway, which today houses the Mellow Mushroom pizza parlor. There was a new name too: The Market Garden. Here, the worker-owners made structural changes inside what at that time had been Schandler's Pickle Barrel, opening walls and the ceiling to create a sense of space. The bakery operations expanded in scope.

Then Stone Soup—or The Market Garden—added a second downtown shop at 8 Wall Street, the location of today's Early Girl Eatery; it did well for a while and then fell victim to the center city's revitalization: lots of restaurants, cafés, coffee shops and bakeries started moving in. National chain restaurants took a bite out of business. Both Stone Soup restaurants closed in 1994.

"Old story: too many choices, too few choosers," Gilbert told the *Asheville Citizen-Times.* "In short, we got out-competed, and the business was no longer viable."

Dick Gilbert, *standing*, got Stone Soup underway. Don Pedi, *seated*. *North Carolina Collection, Pack Memorial Public Library, Asheville, North Carolina.*

Stone Soup while housed at The Manor Inn. *North Carolina Collection, Pack Memorial Public Library, Asheville, North Carolina.*

Today's Mellow Mushroom was once Stone Soup. *Photo by Nan K. Chase.*

The old worker-owners had fond memories of their times at Stone Soup—the early morning hours prepping croutons from day-old bread or the "chicken-pickings" for making chicken broth. Wonderful handcrafted food.

Sandwiches weren't just slapped together; they were "built" from meat and cheese piled high. The Eggstraordinary, for example, consisted of Mary Gilbert's "original egg salad with shaved cream Havarti cheese (dill), tomato, ham and shredded lettuce on sourdough rye bread." That item cost $2.40, or $2.20 with no ham.

The Lotsa Pasta included "pasta spirals, red beans, red onion, chopped tomato, green pepper, egg and grilled chunks of sweet Italian sausage, dressed with a tarragon vinaigrette dressing," according to one restaurant review. The three soups on the menu included a "spicy Tex Mex chili served with corn muffin, lentil soup and soup of the day." The desserts were "decadent."

A generation after it closed, Stone Soup's lasting impact is felt throughout Asheville in the ways the worker-owners influenced a host of community organizations, among them MANNA FoodBank, Slow Food Asheville and the Appalachian Sustainable Agriculture Project.

Graham Yogurt Bread

4 cups whole wheat flour
1 cup unbleached flour
4 teaspoons soda
2 teaspoons salt
4 cups plain yogurt
1 cup molasses
2 cups raisins
1 cup chopped walnuts

Combine dry ingredients in a large mixing bowl. Mix together yogurt, molasses, raisins and nuts. Pour into dry ingredients. Mix well. Divide equally into four small well-greased pans. (Depending on size of pans, you might get six small loaves.) Bake at 350 degrees for 30 minutes or until done. Cool in pan 10 minutes.

Reprinted from *Asheville Citizen-Times*, April 28, 1993

CHAPTER 25

The Windmill European Grill

East Meets West in Downtown Asheville

T he Windmill wasn't just an ethnic restaurant when it opened at 76 Haywood Street in 1984; it was multi-ethnic. Operated by a family that melded French, German and Indian backgrounds, The Windmill European Grill offered Asheville diners a new and exciting menu that combined elements of curry, vindaloo, seafood, sausage and much more.

Of greater importance than The Windmill's delightful and imaginative food was its prominent place in Asheville's evolution from a tourist town with good food to a tourist town based on dining as one of its main attractions—a foodie city.

In addition, one of The Windmill's key personnel, Vijay Shastri, began as a young teenager working with his parents and sister there and quickly started a series of highly regarded restaurants of his own in Asheville. He was one of Asheville's first resident celebrity chefs, working to incorporate local ingredients with out-of-this-world taste combinations, thus inspiring the next generation of culinary stars.

Finally, The Windmill's original location on Haywood Street bridged different eras of the city's development, serving as a pivot point in various battles over commercial development. Haywood Street long has been one of the city's most fashionable shopping districts, but businesses have had to survive huge fluctuations: bustling commercial center, then dead zone and now bustling commercial center again.

An early tenant at 76 Haywood Street, beginning in 1947, was Jimmie's Waffle Shop, which lasted there until 1961. The menu at Jimmie's—open

Home to Windmill European Grill and other restaurants. *North Carolina Collection, Pack Memorial Public Library, Asheville, North Carolina.*

for breakfast, lunch and dinner—included Golden Brown Waffles, steaks and chops, "Old Fashion N. Carolina Barbecue," spaghetti and meatballs, sandwiches and other standard diner fare. The slogan at Jimmie's was "NO BEER—NO WINE—JUST A PLACE TO DINE."

The Windmill eventually moved in but by 1990 was superseded by Vijay Shastri's own Cafe Bombay and then by his Flying Frog Cafe, which later moved to another location on the same block. Beginning shortly after the year 2000, the City of Asheville bought the by then abandoned Flying Frog Cafe building and an adjacent parking facility for future development. Both the building at 76 Haywood Street and the neighboring Handi Park deck were demolished, making way for the next big thing. But bitter political fighting ensued, and today the 0.8-acre site, still owned by the city, remains vacant. Nicknamed the Pit of Despair or "the world's most expensive (non) parking lot" by wags, the sun-soaked gravel expanse is surrounded by a chain link fence but also has picnic tables and umbrellas and serves as an outdoor art space and food truck locale.

But back to The Windmill. A couple named Jay and Cathie (sometimes spelled Kathie) Shastri were the originators; he was a chemist by profession, and his family background was Indian—from India. Her background was French-German by way of Milwaukee, Wisconsin; she was called "the wizard of seasonings" by local writer Carole Currie. The Shastri children, Vijay and Kirti, were thirteen and fourteen years old, respectively, when the restaurant opened, and for Vijay it was a magical existence. While the parents devised their "perfect combination of East and West," as Cathie called it, the kids worked every job in the establishment, learning the restaurant business thoroughly before they were out of high school. In fact, according to one newspaper story, Vijay left high school at 2:00 p.m. every weekday to report to work.

The Windmill almost instantly garnered a favorable review in the *New York Times*, which called it "a very new, very casual downtown restaurant serving some unusual Eastern European specialties."

And still the Shastris continued to ramp up the wow factor at The Windmill. By 1987, Carole Currie was extolling the adventuresome dinner spot, which by now had added rabbit and venison to the menu and was creating everything down to the chutneys in-house:

At the Grill, there's a regular menu with some classics like pork schnitzel and filet mignon (Gypsy Steak) but regulars tend to choose from the specials, of which there are nine or 10 nightly. Cathie's specialty is grilled fish, two or three different ones each day, but what she does with grilled fish is extraordinary. One of her favorites is Norwegian salmon with a light California-style Provencal sauce of chopped tomatoes, garlic, black olives, green onions, olive oil and wine vinegar. Another is a spicy Carolina blue fish dusted with Cajun spices, charcoal broiled and topped with a sauce of cracked black pepper, lemon, sherry wine, oregano and butter.

Cathie's imagination never wearies and she continually creates new combinations. For instance, there's her Chicken Windmill, a chicken breast scaloppini marinated in Greek spices, olive oil and lemon, grilled and topped with a duxelle of artichoke hearts and fresh mushrooms and Greek spices, baked in phyllo dough and topped with a lime Hollandaise....

All the entrees are prepared to order at the Grill. With all but the Indian dinners, diners get sweet and sour red cabbage and a choice of rice pilaf or hot German potato salad, plus fruit garnish. Portions are ample, in the European tradition. The house salad is chopped cucumber and grilled green pepper on greens, topped with feta cheese and a vinaigrette dressing...

I had the Indian dinner ($10.50), Tandoori fish (delicate and delicious Tile fish marinated in Tandoori Masala with Yogurt, coriander, ginger *root, red pepper and Garam Masala spices), charbroiled and topped with chopped onions and radishes, Raita (yogurt with cucumber and cumin seed), Sambar (a hot and spicy curried lentil soup), rice, and Papard, a crisp wafer bread topped with a dollop of chutney. The combinations of hot and cool, soft and crisp were exquisite.*

The dessert menu was equally exotic, and there was an educational angle to every dish. Local reviewer Roni Bea Kayne described The Windmill this way: "This New York–style grill appeals to different tastes because it specializes in Indian foods such as Indian chicken makhanwali and chicken tikka, resmali and samosas, along with European dishes including kielbasa sausage, lamb kabob and fallafel pouri."

By 1990, The Windmill needed bigger quarters to meet customer demand, so the Shastri parents opened The Windmill European Grill/Il Pescatore where the old Bavarian Cellar restaurant had been located, in Innsbruck Mall (see chapter 22), while Vijay and Kirti ran the original Windmill, which by then had morphed into Cafe Bombay. Somehow it seemed natural for a couple of teenagers to run a successful restaurant in Asheville.

Vijay went on to found the Flying Frog Cafe in 1996, also at the 76 Haywood Street location. Later, it moved down the block to 1 Battery Park Avenue. The Flying Frog menu was outrageous, reflecting the deep connection between French and Creole cuisines, plus the German thing: Escargot Maison, Cajun Crawfish Cake, Flying Frog Legs, Stuffed Bayou Oysters, Bierwurst, Chicken Schnitzels, Sauerbraten of Beef and, oh yes, a roast duckling "slow-roasted over a bed of onion & bay leaf; served with a blackberry napoleon brandy sauce with port wine & orange peel," and for dessert Vijay's Chambord Truffle, which was a "Chambord-laced belgian bittersweet chocolate ganache, rolled in walnuts, then dusted with cocoa, cayenne & smoked paprika, served atop a bed of raspberry coulis with a dollop of fresh whipped cream."

Vijay Shastri went on to found Mr. Frog's Soul and Creole Kitchen, which was located in the old Ritz Restaurant building (see chapter 8), and, most recently, Shastri's Continental Lounge at 77 Biltmore Avenue in downtown Asheville.

CHAPTER 26

Laurey's Gourmet Comfort Food

"Joy on the Menu"

There are still a few of the old bumper stickers around Asheville that say "Don't Postpone Joy" in bold blue lettering on a white background. They used to be all over town, stuck onto cars belonging to happy customers of Laurey's Gourmet Comfort Food, at 67 Biltmore Avenue.

Every "Don't Postpone Joy" bumper sticker still out there represents a bit of Laurey Masterton's legacy of joyful living even in the midst of tragedy and hardship.

Laurey's Gourmet Comfort Food—sometimes operating under slightly different, more complicated, names—made its mark on downtown Asheville's late twentieth-century restaurant comeback scene not so much because of the food (although it was hearty, fresh and delicious) but because of Laurey's big-hearted personality and her immense contributions to Asheville's humanitarian organizations. Her powerful and positive spirit inspired everyone who worked alongside her or ate at her increasingly popular café or took home dinner from her grab-and-go deli.

By the time Laurey died, in 2014 at age fifty-nine, she had already battled cancer three times—uterine cancer at age twenty-five, ovarian cancer at thirty-four and colon cancer in her mid-fifties—before finally succumbing. Along the way, she became a cancer activist as well as a cookbook author, a prime mover in Asheville's "cook local" scene, a nationally recognized healthy-food advocate, a potent fundraiser and a TED Talk veteran, as well as a board member of several national

Laurey Masterton poses proudly at Laurey's. *North Carolina Collection, Pack Memorial Public Library, Asheville, North Carolina.*

organizations. Laurey bicycled more than three thousand miles across the United States to raise cancer awareness, and late in life she hiked for thirty-five days on Spain's Camino de Santiago de Compostela pilgrimage route.

To say that Laurey Masterton had it rough would be an understatement; she had it rotten. Yet she gave and gave and gave, always challenging herself by setting and meeting big goals.

Both of Laurey's parents died of cancer in 1996, when she was twelve years old, one in July, the other in October. John and Elsie Masterton had started the famed Blueberry Hill Farm in Vermont, so Laurey grew up around serious cooking, and cooking had been a way to stay close to her mother's memory. After her parents' deaths, she and her two older sisters "farmed themselves out to other families, ending up at boarding schools and college," according to a news account. Laurey studied lighting design and worked Off-Broadway (and Off-Off-Broadway) before chucking it all and moving to Asheville.

At that time, in 1987, the Biltmore Avenue section of downtown Asheville was still "Deadville," Laurey told a reporter for the *Asheville Post*. She told another writer she had seen tumbleweed blowing down the street, which was known as a failed commercial zone gone to seed; open prostitution and X-rated movie houses still operated, and property crime was rife. The *Mountain Xpress* newspaper called "most of Asheville still degenerate." But there was something about the place she liked...

Laurey had a small apartment, and without any business background, she started a catering enterprise out of her kitchen. That was illegal, and three years later, "she got busted by the health department," according to the *Asheville Post*. It was time to get real.

Her catering business was starting to flourish, so she got a tiny storefront at 60 Biltmore Avenue, today the home of Lola Salon & Gallery. There was seating for four, plus the catering kitchen. She added more seats but still needed to expand.

That's when the move across the street took place, to 67 Biltmore Avenue. Laurey occupied part of a well-proportioned one-story building by one of Asheville's Gilded Age architects, Richard Sharp Smith, that had been used as a storage barn for old city trolley cars. Over the years, she expanded, notably taking over the sunny space next door, awash in midday light.

Laurey's concept was comfort food, gourmet comfort food, because she certainly knew the solace that a meal could bring. She offered delicious meals to order ahead for pickup, and that was a hit with working people who were short on time. Once she had expanded the restaurant, there was also room to dine in, and customers loved the upbeat, informal atmosphere. For a while, the restaurant went by the name Laurey's Catering and Gourmet-to-Go.

The weekly menu at Laurey's featured a different dinner to go every day (order by noon, pick up by 3:00 p.m.), such fare as Honey-Thyme Roasted Chicken with Leeks and Carrots, Bistro Steak with Rosemary Potato Gratin, Braised Local Lamb with Wilted Greens and Cumin Spiced Shrimp Skewers over Southwestern Rice. The dine-in lunch menu offered sandwiches and salads and yummy baked-on-site cookies.

Laurey Masterton of Laurey's. *Courtesy of Storey Publishing.*

The closer Laurey got to the end of her life, the more driven she became to grow and share. She was a skilled beekeeper and wore a necklace holding a tiny vial; inside was a single drop of honey representing the life's output of one bee.

When she wrote a honey-based cookbook, *The Fresh Honey Cookbook*, she tackled the subject with her typical thoroughness, grouping recipes by month and meal and featuring different kinds of honey.

"She had a heart of gold," one friend observed in the *Asheville Citizen-Times* after Laurey's death. "She also made stuff happen."

The restaurant, which Laurey herself was calling Café*Catering*Comfort at the end, continued to operate for about a year after her death. Her sisters decided to step away from any involvement and finally closed Laurey's Café and Catering. Today, the retail space is occupied by a thriving catering business, 67 Biltmore, which has drawn on Laurey's guiding principles of fresh local food lovingly prepared.

Here is Laurey's recipe called Dolce e Forte, meaning "sweet and strong," from *The Fresh Honey Cookbook*. It's a savory topping to spread on slices of toasted slightly stale baguette—or on anything else interesting.

Dolce e Forte

1 cup pancetta, roughly chopped
1 cup pine nuts
1 cup golden raisins
½ brined capers, drained
½ cup candied orange peel (optional)
4 tablespoons butter
1 teaspoon unbleached all-purpose flour
2 tablespoons honey, preferably sourwood honey
6 tablespoons distilled white vinegar
Baguette, sliced diagonally ½ inch thick

Combine the pancetta, pine nuts, raisins, capers, and candied peel, if using, in a food grinder or food processor. Pulse a few times until the mixture is the consistency of ham salad. Be careful not to make it too fine.

Combine the butter, flour, and honey in a medium skillet. Cook over medium heat until it starts to foam.

Add 3 tablespoons water and the vinegar to the skillet. Cook for 2 minutes to unite the ingredients. Stir in the pancetta mixture and cook for just 1 minute longer. It will be a thick, spreadable mixture.

Spread on the sliced baguette. Serve as is. Or, if you like, preheat the broiler. Place the slices on a baking sheet and broil for 1 to 2 minutes, just until it toasts.

In beer-happy Asheville, it's nice to remember a traditional nonalcoholic beverage to enjoy on a hot summer day. Rosemary Lemonade with Sage Honey, from *The Fresh Honey Cookbook*, is the real deal, using honey rather than sugar.

Rosemary Lemonade with Sage Honey
(Serves 12)

½ cup honey, preferably sage honey
16 fresh rosemary sprigs
12 lemons (to make about 2 cups juice)

To make a simple syrup, combine the honey and ½ cup water in a small saucepan and bring to a boil over high heat.

Turn off the heat. While the syrup is still hot, add 4 of the rosemary sprigs and let steep in the syrup until the syrup is at room temperature. Remove the rosemary and place in your compost pile.

Squeeze the lemons. Combine the lemon juice with the warm rosemary syrup. Add 8 cups water to the mixture.

To serve, fill each glass with ice and then pour the mixture into each glass. Add a sprig of the remaining fresh rosemary to each glass.

CHAPTER 27

Magnolia's Raw Bar & Grille

It's a Party

The weather would be sweltering. July or August, depending on the year. If you had to settle for an outdoor perch along the street-side planter boxes, the sun beat down mercilessly at that western corner of pavement—North Market and Walnut Streets—in late afternoon, and the press of the crowd added to the heat. The upside? You could watch the performance for free.

If you got a table indoors in the shaded courtyard of Magnolia's, called the Garden Patio, the conditions might still be hot and humid in the extreme, but no one dared give up a coveted seat and the food and beverage service that went with it. However, when seated indoors, you risked making eye contact with the headline performer, the Reverend Billy C. Wirtz. And if that happened, you could quickly end up the butt of some very clever, very cutting verses. All in good fun, naturally, and lots of laughs. But…ouch. There was no escape.

Such was the long-running Asheville street festival known as Bele Chere, which began in 1979 as a desperate attempt to get people to come downtown and spend some money and ended in 2013 because the festival became such a mob scene that downtown merchants were begging for its demise so business could return to what had become a dull roar by then. "Beautiful living." That was the made-up French phrase for the Bele Chere festival. Lots of free music, plus food, beer and craft vendors—Bele Chere.

The Reverend Billy C. Wirtz was part of the scene, a talented, energetic, whack job of an entertainer—bawdy songster and marvelous keyboard player on his amped-up ivories. And Magnolia's Raw Bar & Grille was his spot for years and years, beginning in 1988, when the restaurant first opened. Reverend Billy was good for two four-hour sets over two days of Bele Chere.

Magnolia's Raw Bar & Grille was the restaurant version of a grandchild, in this case the grandchild of Peterson's Grill, an old Asheville favorite. Brothers Nick and Gus Peterson started the grill about 1947 just around the corner, having opened an earlier diner twenty years before that (chapter 11 of this book provides details). Two of their grandsons, Chris and Nick Peterson, started Magnolia's in 1988, a pivotal period in the renaissance of downtown Asheville as a tourist destination. The commercial zone was still substantially boarded up, and businesspeople investing downtown were seen as gutsy—maybe crazy—pioneers.

A complimentary opening review in the *Asheville Citizen-Times* explained the appeal:

> *Magnolia's is attractive, uptown, jazzy, and the food is full of adventure.*
>
> *Magnolia's is almost like three different restaurants in one. If you eat on the covered garden patio, it feels like New Orleans, with plants and wrought iron surrounding the breezy courtyard. The Magnolia Room inside has the air of Charleston propriety, softened with carpet, peachy colors and prints and paintings of southern scenes covering the walls. And the raw bar and grille has the chatty, informal atmosphere of an Atlanta pub.*
>
> *The restaurant is the brainchild of Nick and Chris Peterson, owners of the next door nightclub, Cinjades's, and 45 Cherry, who had been wanting to get into the restaurant business with a first class operation. The two spent many thousands in a dramatic and imaginative redo of building space that included the former McArthur-Krause florist shop and the adjacent parking lot (now the garden patio)....*
>
> *Seafood gets a big emphasis and in fact, the raw oysters on the half shell are sold by the bushels. Another popular dish has been a considerably more dressed-up seafood, Tuna Madagascar, grilled tuna with a delicate green peppercorn and shrimp sauce.*

In those early days of the downtown Asheville rebirth Magnolia's menu represented a big step up from the usual diner fare and included such alluring dishes as blue crab ravioli and tomato concasse; grilled Norwegian salmon with lobster and melted leeks; grilled sea bass with salmon mousse and new potatoes, snow peas and fiddlehead ferns; plus a mixed seafood grill with Dijon sauce (grill species included "tuna, amberjack and halibut,"

The quiet scene today where Magnolia's customers once partied. *Photo by Nan K. Chase.*

the newspaper reported). There were heaps of crab legs and boiled shrimp to peel and eat, or fried oyster po'boy sandwiches. And the desserts were decadent: "Mandarin Chocolate Torte, a sponge cake soaked in Cointreau and spread with orange marmalade, then frosted with a whipped chocolate frosting and served on a chocolate crème Anglais." Like that.

Magnolia's wasn't just about the food and drink, though. Right from the start, management liked to bring in live entertainment and support Asheville's budding performance scene. In 1988, for example, Magnolia's teamed up with the Asheville Community Theater, located directly across Walnut Street, for a festive luau-themed preview party before the opening of Rodgers and Hammerstein's musical *South Pacific*. The $18.95 (or $19.95, depending on the source) price of the "lavish buffet" luau, taking place at 5:00 p.m., included admission to the show at 7:30. The luau menu featured coconut shrimp, roast pork and spiced coconut-scallop soup. Magnolia's also sponsored several sneak peeks of *South Pacific* that season; for $5.00, patrons could enjoy a few selections from the play sung by cast members at the restaurant.

Even when nothing special was going on, Magnolia's managed to keep the fun alive and garner press coverage in the process. In 2001, a tender-hearted customer, college junior R.H. Temple, brought his girlfriend in for dinner, and they noticed an enormous lobster in the cold-water tank—a real monster that weighed in at nine pounds, as opposed to a normal-size lobster of a pound or two. "My girlfriend felt really sorry for it," the young man told feature writer John Boyle of the *Asheville Citizen-Times*.

So the chivalrous swain paid to liberate the lobster and take it to Maine for release (what college student wouldn't give that a whirl?). The market rate would have been $130, but Magnolia's management cut him a deal: half price. Temple bought the lobster and kept it alive, properly chilled and oxygenated, for several weeks in his dorm room at nearby Brevard College. The big challenge was transporting it; Temple loaded the lobster and his dogs—four pit bulls—into his pickup truck and drove twenty-six hours to Acadia National Park, where he muscled his way through four feet of snow and got the lobster into the sea. Long, tense minutes ensued until the lobster got acclimated to open water.

"Once he got used to the water, he headed out there to a pile of rocks," Temple told the *Citizen-Times*. "When it was walking out in the water and it was healthy and everything, it was all worth it."

No matter how outlandish the party atmosphere, the food at Magnolia's was always a serious endeavor, thanks to its owners' Greek culinary roots and long exposure to the restaurant business. The younger Peterson brothers had first spent years operating Peterson Amusement Co., a local enterprise with pinball machines and bowling lanes. In 1984, they took a chance on the downtown Asheville development trend, however, and opened a dance club called Cinjade's in a former carriage house next door to what would become Magnolia's. There was a certain amount of crossover between the two businesses, and eventually things got prickly, as sometimes happens with family.

A 2013 *Asheville Citizen-Times* account titled "Cinjade's Nightclub Fades to Black" explained that owner Chris Peterson wanted to slow down as he neared retirement age. He would still operate Magnolia's. But suddenly in 2018, Magnolia's closed under murky circumstances; the staff "walked out en masse," according to an Ashvegas online report, or perhaps Peterson himself forced a shutdown. No matter the cause, the end had come, and the location soon became home to an upscale destination called Brasilia Churrasco Steakhouse.

One other thing about Magnolia's. Thanks to owner Chris Peterson's wholehearted and vocal pro-business, anti-government philosophy, the restaurant was often the site of Republican post-election parties and was also known for its support of the local Council for Independent Business Owners. Nothing's simple in Asheville.

CHAPTER 28

Ristorante da Vincenzo

Opera Tragicomica

I t's a good thing that online diner reviews didn't exist when Ristorante da Vincenzo opened, early in 1991, because the place might not have lasted as long as it did, which was 2015. By then the reviews—freewheeling internet tirades rather than well-modulated newspaper accounts, as before— were mostly brutal, but they made for droll reading and there were still a few genuinely enthusiastic postings.

Vincenzo's started out *bada bing bada boom* with a real Italian chef, Vincenzo Tito, brought over near the end of his successful career as a restaurant owner in Milan, Italy, to cook authentic northern Italian specialties in Asheville. Tito was recruited informally. According to one Asheville native, now a restaurateur herself, "My mother's fourth husband, his ex-wife, was an airline stewardess, and she had an uncle in Italy that they wanted to bring over. And it was phenomenal food."

The restaurant's owners also had a great location, at 10 North Market Street, in an interesting building that was formerly the city morgue and more recently the first home of The Market Place Restaurant, which is still a city favorite but now on Wall Street. The building had a playful Dutch Rococo style executed in fancy brickwork and decorative painting outside and "lush and romantic floral prints for the table coverings and window treatments" inside, according to an early review in the *Asheville Citizen-Times*. There was even a parking lot with eighteen spaces, a choice amenity in downtown Asheville.

Vincenzo's mural and sign still grace the building. *Photo by Nan K. Chase.*

The owners added a lively complement of entertainment with singers and instrumentalists, food and wine events, holiday celebrations and the like. "The restaurant will join the Cinjade's nightclub and Magnolia's restaurant on the beautiful brick section of North Market between College and Walnut," the newspaper announced in December 1990.

In the two-story Vincenzo's, the lower level would serve as the informal venue for such uses as a cigar bar, a piano bar, an espresso bar, a Scotch and tequila bar and a "chic and trendy lunch spot" with bargain pasta specials, while the dining room upstairs was more formal—including, for a while, a harpist playing "classical, pop, folk and new age music."

And the timing was good for the opening of Vincenzo's. By 1991, the worst of the dead years were over for downtown Asheville, and while the central business district still looked pretty beat up from decades of neglect and decay, enough cultural events were churning now that opening a restaurant didn't look quite so insane.

One of the original Vincenzo's owners was Chris Peterson—cue the dark and dramatic entrance music—who was also involved at that time in two neighboring businesses: Magnolia's Raw Bar & Grille (see chapter 26) and Cinjade's nightclub. Peterson sold his part-interest in Vincenzo's restaurant operations in 1992 but continued owning the building.

In the end, it was a long-simmering landlord dispute that closed Vincenzo's. The restaurant's owner since 1996, an original Vincenzo's waiter named Dwight Butner, eventually lost his lease—in full view of the local press and the dining public. Peterson done him in.

Chris Peterson could charitably be described as combative, and newspaper coverage of his long career in public affairs has been more than a little amusing. The guy loved his First Amendment right to outrage anyone within hearing range.

"I feel like I'm running against everybody," Peterson said in October 1991 while he was campaigning for a seat on the Asheville City Council. "Personally, I'd like to be elected and I feel like I'm running against everybody."

Even as an elected official, Peterson was ejected from council chambers more than once: he "was thrown out of an Asheville city council meeting for loudly protesting the possible removal of *Playboy* magazine from city newsstands," according to the *Citizen-Times*, and later, as reported in the *Mountain Xpress* newspaper, he was escorted out for insisting to Mayor Esther Manheimer that the city budget was a 'Ponzi scheme.'"

In 1992, during the early years of Asheville's Bele Chere festival, the city's fire chief had the nerve to cite Peterson at his Magnolia's establishment for overcrowding and for having "obstructed and locked fire exits."

As for the food at Vincenzo's, the menu started out under Vincenzo Tito's close supervision to specialize in chicken, veal, seafood and beef entrées, light salads and antipasti, plus rich pasta dishes (Lasagna Forno "to die for," raved early restaurant partner Anna Slosman). Tito, however, left the stage after just a year or so.

Making an appearance around 1994 was a female chef, rare at the time, who had chucked her earlier life in Ohio to concentrate on her own vision. Susan Gary, "a chef with no formal training," as the *Citizen-Times* emphasized, liked to dabble in mash-ups like elk meat with dates and figs and such:

A little bit peasant oriented, with field greens and sautéed spinach… casual…whimsical.…Crispy risotto cakes filled with cheese, smoked trout mousse and eggplant and garlic pastry, steamed mussels…served with fresh herbs and garlic…homemade wild mushroom paste served with a roasted garlic and tomato sauce…roasted tenderloin of beef specially ordered and meltingly tender.

Exit stage left.

Then chef Daniel "Woody" Desmond took center stage, pleasing customers, at least for a while, with creamy, herb-saturated meals. Artichoke hearts, red snapper, olives and olive oil, garlic and lemons, fennel, cannelloni.…

Ristorante da Vincenzo menu, in one of various spellings. *North Carolina Collection, Pack Memorial Public Library, Asheville, North Carolina.*

The problem was, well, apparently the landlord's reluctance to modernize the structure. Cue the weeping.

By 2013, the *Asheville Citizen-Times* was reporting that restaurant owner Dwight Butner's relations with Peterson "had been tense" of late, with both men embroiled in legal wrangling that might end up in court.

And by now, internet restaurant reviews were gaining momentum, unfortunately for Vincenzo's. An early Yelp critique read:

> *Both dishes suffered from an egregiously heavy handed dose of garlic. I mean whoa.*
>
> *You may be thinking, I like garlic, that's not a bad thing, but let me tell you, I have never tasted such garlic in my life! And being an Italian lady who tends to quadruple the amount of garlic in all recipes, that is something. I think it took me until after breakfast this morning before I could erase the aftertaste of raw garlic from my mouth! I mean whoa.*

The website Dirty Spoon shared a scathing anonymous review of Vincenzo's cast as an opera in four acts.

> *The arborio is painfully dry. Truly. Parboiled rice dry. The large capped mushrooms poke out like mountain peaks among the nearly crispy grains. There is also so much freshly chopped parsley garnishing the dish that it makes the entire plate green. With each forkful, the few grains of arborio look like children tumbling down a giant grassy, herby knoll....*
>
> *Atop the firm, lumpy, underwhelming excuse for potato dumplings, sit thin slices of prosciutto (possessing equally thin ribbons of fat) and scallions (for some reason)....*
>
> *I'm not sure when Vincenzo's hit its sweet spot, but I imagine that as long as it has been around, it must have been something special. It hangs in the air here, glancing down from the chandeliers, like a ghost just wanting to play again.*

By 2014, public rumors about lease problems began surfacing, and reviews trended savage.

Vincenzo's closed in February 2015. Today, the space houses Polanco Restaurant, a Mexican-themed eatery run by an Anglo guy from Illinois. The old brick-paved street is worth a visit.

CHAPTER 29

La Caterina Trattoria

Angels Overhead

Downtown Asheville's dining scene revved up around 1995, with new restaurants opening every year, on every block. The energy was terrific. People were back, filling the sidewalks and brightening up the nights that had been so dark and dreary for so long.

La Caterina Trattoria opened in 1994 on Pack Square, and the joie de vivre plus the cooking chops of owners Victor and Robbin Giancola may have provided the crucial spark, both from a food and wine standpoint and in their rah-rah Asheville boosterism. La Caterina brought fine dining to town, but in a friendly way.

The restaurant, tucked into a narrow storefront at 5 Pack Square, had a big pasta-making machine displayed in the front window. At night, subtly lit, the scene looked like an Edward Hopper painting, quiet and pastel; by day, that pasta machine stayed busy. Inside the dining room, a beautiful mural of cherubs graced the ceiling, and opera music was always playing in the background. The atmosphere was intimate, like a neighborhood trattoria on a side street in Italy. La Caterina Trattoria was perhaps the first of the downtown restaurants to feature outdoor patio seating, just like in the old country.

The food was out of this world, thanks to Victor Giancola's culinary roots in New York City. That's where he learned to dry and cure meats, to make wine-cured sausage and pancetta and cheeses like ricotta and mozzarella. And that's what he and his wife, Robbin, served up so graciously in Asheville. They made everything in-house, with the ravioli often selling out first. The extensive game menu was unusual, serving as a foil for savory sauces.

La Caterina Trattoria took off like a rocket because of that food. No one could beat it. The portions were generous and the pricing reasonable, the presentation on point: white linen, wine in small tumblers and an endless supply of crusty baguette slices and seasoned olive oil. The Giancolas wanted a night on the town to be easy yet special, not a budget buster, and they got lucky with a talented young chef, Damien Cavicchi, who would go on to become an executive chef at the Biltmore Estate.

Early on, lunch service included a lunch cart for quick selections of "interesting salads or a huge wedge of sandwich, made with focaccia bread," according to an early *Asheville Citizen-Times* review.

Dinner was ever-changing, with the day's menu posted on a chalkboard. Three years into the business, another rapturous review described some of the offerings: "pasta, fish, chicken and veal…maybe rabbit ragu on pappardelle one night and braciole, thinly sliced sirloin rolled with Italian bacon, Romano cheese and herbs another." Of the salad: "The arugula was covered with garlic toasted walnuts, gorgonzola and vinaigrette— wonderful and more than enough for two to share." Of the "salmon fillet with brown garlic butter on a bed of spinach, served with a side of spaghetti and marinara" the verdict read, "The salmon was moist and flaky. In the risotto, a creamy rice dish, the chunks of squash were perfectly cooked and a marvelous addition to the entrees."

When La Caterina Trattoria threw a traditional Easter dinner in 1998, the menu for this "Banchetto di Pasquale" included "an Easter torte filled with Italian chesses and cold cuts, spinach salad with walnuts and orange vinaigrette, chicken soup with couscous, pasta with chick peas, artichoke hearts and mint, entrée of pork roast with garlic mustard or roasted leg of lamb, and fried fish served with lemon. For dessert—Panna cotta with mixed berries."

Chef Damien told a *Citizen-Times* writer, "A lot of people think every [Italian] restaurant should serve fettuccine Alfredo and veal parmigiana, red sauce goes with everything, and there should be a big bottle of Chianti on every table. All those things are NOT what I'm about."

Exactly. His menu for La Caterina's ninth anniversary dinner included "sweet pea flan with crabmeat and fennel salad; spinach pasta filled with roasted rabbit and ricotta served with braised carrot and chive oil; veal braciole with tuna sauce; and risotto with lamb and roasted tomato vinaigrette. Dessert will be lemon panna cotta with blueberries and honey." One newspaper photo showed him filleting a thirty-pound grouper—a bold move.

For the eleventh annual Christmas dinner, the Notte di Sette Pesci (Night of Seven Fishes), the five-course meal would feature "baccala (salt cod), clams, octopus, shrimp, calamari, tuna and scallops."

An everyday menu listed such unusual pasta dishes as Spaghetti Carciofe con Anatra ("Fresh baby artichoke hearts sautéed with slow roasted duck meat tossed with spaghetti") and Palli Angelli e Piselli ("Tiny chicken meatballs and peas in tomato broth with pappardelle"). The garlic soup was outstanding, and one brunch menu included Nest of the Dove (capellini pasta with a poached egg resting in the middle, adorned with shaved prosciutto and finished with a "light cream sauce").

Victor and Robbin liked any excuse to throw a party, not just for the food and drink but also for the chance to help the community. Thus their support for fundraising events; beneficiaries included the Animal Compassion Network, the March of Dimes, Eliada Home, the Asheville Art Museum, the Asheville Tourists baseball team and a couple of Biltmore Village restaurants that were flooded out by Hurricane Frances in 2004.

La Caterina Trattoria honored family and friends. *North Carolina Collection, Pack Memorial Public Library, Asheville, North Carolina.*

Piccolo Piatti	Insalate	Pesce

Piccolo Piatti

Melanzane Involtini - Grilled eggplant rolls stuffed with goat cheese, roasted red peppers & basil 6.50

Mozzarella - In-house made, served with caponata 5.50

Insalata Polpo - Grilled baby octopus on potato-fennel salad 7.95

Gamberi al Forno - Large shrimp roasted in iron skillet with garlic, olive oil, and lemon 8.95

Mussels Posillipo - Mussels steamed with wine, tomato and garlic 6.95

Gnocchi - Potato gnocchi with sorrel pesto 5.95

Carde Repiene en Brodo - Swiss chard stuffed with ricotta and poached in chicken broth 5.50

Antipasti Salumi - Assorted in-house cured meats, aged provolone, olives and giardiniera 6.50

Salsicce al Forno - In-house made sausage on baked polenta with roasted tomato, olives and provolone 5.50

Stone Oven Pizza

Margherita - In-house made mozzarella, tomatoes and basil 6.95

Salsicce - In-house made sausage, marinara and provolone 6.95

Patate - Thinly sliced potato and gorgonzola 6.95

Giuseppe - Cremini mushrooms, carmelized onions, smoked mozzarella and guanciale 8.95

Insalate

Mixed Greens- Garlic toasted walnuts, gorgonzola, grape tomatoes & lemon vinaigrette 6.50

Caesar- romaine, garlic croutons & romano 6.50

Bresaola - Wine-cured, air dried beef sliced thin on greens with horseradish vinaigrette 7.95

Pasta

Ravioli - In-house made, filled with ricotta, romano and mint. With marinara or bolognese 14.50

Penne Pastore - Tossed with sausage, sautéed greens and ricotta 13.25

Spaghetti Carciofe con Anatra - Fresh baby artichoke hearts sautéed with slow roasted duck meat tossed with spaghetti 15.95

Spaghetti Carbonara - Tossed with in-house cured pancetta, green peas, egg & romano 13.95

Manicotti Spinache - In-house made spinach manicotti filled with ricotta and spinach and baked in a light tomato sauce 14.50

Palli Angelli e Piselli - Tiny chicken meatballs and peas in tomato broth with pappardelle 13.95

Linguine con Pesto - Tossed with basil-walnut pesto 11.95

Agnolotti Manzo - In-house made, filled with braised beef & tossed with mushrooms & spinach in a light truffled cream sauce 16.95

Lasagne - In-house made pasta layered with ricotta, mozzarella, bolognese and balsamella 14.50

Pasta Verdure - Sautéed vegetable of the day tossed with choice of pasta 12.95

An 18% service charge will be added to the check for parties of 6 or more.

Pesce

Salmon - Stone oven roasted and served on spinach-potato frittata 20.95

Trout - Boneless locally raised trout with hazelnut pesto and prosciutto. Served with wild mushroom grano (prosciutto optional) 18.95

Puttanesca - Shrimp and assorted fresh fish of the day sautéed in tomato sauce seasoned with kalamata olives, capers, & white wine. Served on cappellini 18.95

Carne

Breast of Duckling - Seared, sliced thin with marsala glaze. With sautéed spinach and wild mushroom grano 17.95

Salsicce del Giorno - In-house made sausage of the day (ask server for preparation) 14.95

Pollo Argento - Grilled, boneless chicken breast with red pepper pesto and melted provolone. Served with pasta 15.95

Ragu Coniglio - Rabbit and walnut stew served on grano 16.95

Lamb Shank - Braised with marsala and wild mushrooms. Served on soft polenta 15.95

Casseruola Braciole Maiale - Pork braciole baked with cannellini beans, tomato and eggplant 14.95

Ossobuco - Veal shank braised in tomato and white wine, topped with gremolata & served with saffron risotto 20.95

New York Strip (12 oz.) - Grilled, dry aged Prime beef topped with local mushrooms and herb butter. Served with Patate Pepe 24.95

Colli di Manzo (for two) - Bone-in, dry aged Prime ribeye oven roasted with dry marinade & served in cast iron skillet. Served with Patate Pepe 42.95

The mouthwatering menu at La Caterina Trattoria. *North Carolina Collection, Pack Memorial Public Library, Asheville, North Carolina.*

La Caterina had no room to expand either the kitchen or the dining room on Pack Square, so in 1998 the Giancolas grew sideways by opening Il Paradiso Steak and Chop House, a second restaurant, at 39 Elm Street. This location was almost impossible to find, next to the Merrimon Avenue freeway exit ramp from I-240, and although the initial reviews were glowing—such tender steaks and so much elegant space—a rotation of chefs began, and the end was in sight. Reviews tanked.

When Il Paradiso closed, at the end of 2003, La Caterina Trattoria soon moved from Pack Square to take over those spacious quarters. But even with Damien Cavicchi back at the helm, the owners couldn't make it work. They had already opened a new restaurant, the short-lived Potenza, in nearby Hendersonville. La Caterina closed for good in 2008, having elevated the standard of Asheville dining.

Today, the restaurant Rhubarb has overtaken La Caterina's Pack Square presence, while a new hotel is rising at the Elm Street locale.

The *Asheville Citizen-Times* published Damien Cavicchi's recipe for lamb chops while he was executive chef at La Caterina Trattoria.

Braciole Agnello

1 ½ pounds trimmed lamb leg
3 cups breadcrumbs (rustic bread such as ciabatta)
1 ounce chopped fresh mint
2 ounces pistachios, coarsely ground
Zest of one orange, minced
½ cup grated pecorino Romano
3 quarts lamb stock, veal stock or chicken broth (may be store bought)
2 cups red table wine
Sea salt
Red pepper flakes
⅔ cup good quality olive oil (divided)

Cut the lamb into 3 ounce pieces and place each piece between two sheets of plastic film.

With a meat mallet, pound gently until very thin, like scallopini. Combine breadcrumbs, mint, pistachios, orange zest, ⅓ cup olive oil and Romano.

Add red pepper flakes to taste.

Lay out the lamb scallopini and evenly distribute the bread crumb mixture. Roll the lamb, being careful to tuck in the sides so as not to allow any filling to escape.

Arrange the braciole snugly into a casserole dish lightly oiled with olive oil and season with salt.

Place into a pre-heated 450 degree oven for 25 minutes or until richly browned.

Once browned, remove and reduce heat to 350 degrees. Pour wine over braciole and dislodge any braciole and brown bits that have stuck to the pan. Add lamb stock (or substitute), salt and red pepper flakes. Cover, and return to oven for 1 hour.

Serve with sautéed broccoli, rabe or escarole.

Serves 4.

CHAPTER 30

Burgermeister's

Biggest, Best Burgers

You didn't have to be a meat lover to love Burgermeister's, a mostly local hangout renowned for its huge, innovative beef hamburgers and leaner elk burgers and bison burgers, as well as for its flavorful veggie burgers, its homemade mayonnaise and roasted garlic–infused ketchup and spicy mustard, its freshly baked Kaiser buns, its crunchy-licious deep-fried pickle slices served with zesty homemade ranch dressing, its rich seafood gumbo, its over-the-top grilled cheese sandwiches whether the calendar said Grilled Cheese Month (April) or not, its herby potato and sweet potato wedges, its ginger iced tea and, in later years, its "adult milkshakes," which were regular ice cream or fruit milkshakes spiked with such liqueurs as Kahlua, Jägermeister, Grand Marnier and Butterscotch Schnapps. Okay, so peanut butter ice cream isn't "regular," but it worked.

Talk about decadent. You could really stuff your face and then wipe off the grease and take home leftovers for later. Diets went to die at Burgermeister's.

In its first iteration, Burgermeister's New Orleans Grill opened in 1995 and was located in a tiny storefront at 3 South Pack Square, in the heart of downtown Asheville. The place was so small that in the beginning there was only counter service and a few stools, although management was able to grow the business by offering takeout and also weekday lunch deliveries downtown and by adding outdoor seating under a colorful awning. And cooks at home could call up and order the uncooked burger patties—and roasted garlic bread—already made up to grill on the patio. The food was a hit.

Or as an *Asheville Citizen-Times* retrospective of the Asheville burger scene declared, "Burgermeister's ruled the roost in downtown Asheville."

A few years later, Burgermeister's closed as the owners sought other business opportunities (spoiler alert: veggie burger production) but in 2003 reopened in West Asheville (not yet "*trendy*" West Asheville") as Burgermeister's Kitchen and Tap, in a compact strip-mall location with a wall of windows, the better for people watching: 697-A Haywood Road, once the home of Ms. Kasey's Soul Food. The "eclectic" Burgermeister's décor on Haywood Road had plenty of seating and featured race car and professional wrestling memorabilia, paintings on velvet, old show cards from indie music concerts and all manner of vintage photo advertisements.

Burgermeister's offered something special for late-night concert-goers with the munchies: the kitchen stayed open until 1:00 a.m. on Friday and Saturday nights, with the dining area remaining open until 2:00 a.m.

From the start, both Burgermeister's locations served beer. In a bit of reverse snobbism, the downtown café sold domestic beers only—think PBR for six dollars a pitcher—while the West Asheville place was also able to offer beers from Asheville's emerging local brewing industry. Nice.

The Burgermeister's hamburgers were described in various newspaper and online reviews in terms like "incredibly tall," "two-handed," "so big you can barely get your mouth around 'em," "big, fatty burgers, not for the faint of heart," "truly one-of-a-kind" and just plain "amazing."

In Asheville's rapidly evolving culinary landscape, Burgermeister's was known for innovation in a few specialty areas, mostly burger related. The chef there was among the first in town to concentrate on elevating hamburgers from frozen flat-top horrors to a food with flair, now starting to be called the "haute hamburger."

In an *Asheville Citizen-Times* "history of the Asheville burger," Chantal Saunders, who was part owner of the West Asheville Burgermeister's for a time, called burgers "the new black," adding, "A hamburger could be a McDonald's burger or the $200 truffle and Kobe burger. It's a great, neutral vehicle for creative expression."

The go-to burger at Burgermeister's was called The Meister: nine ounces of smoked ground beef marinated in Guinness stout and Worcestershire sauce before being grilled to perfection. Toppings included caramelized onions and marinated tomatoes. Price: $6.95.

There were about a dozen equally elaborate burgers on the menu, several of them vegetarian. The Burgermeister's owners were serious about devising the best veggie burgers ever—experimenting with almost forty food combinations to achieve a balance of flavor, texture, moistness and nutrition. That would be the VeggieMeister's World's Greatest Veggie Burger, to which effort Burgermeister's owners, Dan Watts and his good buddy Smith "Smitty" Gaddy, devoted several years and unknown funds but which seems to have sunk like a stone. A second Gaddy brother, Tom, came aboard on the West Asheville operation and was married for a while to Chantal Saunders.

Burgermeister's approach to food was gung-ho, and the menu expanded to include Asheville throw-downs like a Carolina crab cake sandwich, a marinated grilled portabella sandwich, a tofu Philly sub, a shrimp po'boy, an open-faced turkey-Mex sandwich ("oven roasted turkey with french fries on toast, queso cheese & pico de gallo") and an even more intense pork chop sandwich ("fried pork chop topped with an egg, lettuce, tomato, caramelized onions and mayo on a bun"), and for dessert a strawberry-maple and blackberry-ginger custard. Care for an adult milkshake to wash that down?

Yo, and the "basil and fennel sausage for the gumbo" was also made in-house.

Of course, as an upstanding member of Asheville's fast-growing independent restaurant network, called AIR, Burgermeister's participated in a number of fundraising and other worthy efforts: for culinary scholarships at Asheville-Buncombe Technical Community College's stellar training program, for the American Red Cross and for green energy retrofits.

In the last years, cracks appeared in Burgermeister's reputation, online and elsewhere. One word said it all: "awful." The restaurant closed in 2013, followed by a short run by The Barleycorn, billed as a gastropub after extensive interior upgrades.

Today, the bright and beautiful BimBeriBon at 697-A Haywood Street serves up quinoa oat waffles, wild mushroom toast and, perhaps in a nod to Burgermeister's, sweet potato fries.

BURGERMEISTER'S FETA-SESAME BURGER WAS A customer favorite. The *Asheville Citizen-Times* shared the recipe on July 4, 2008 after it originally appeared in *Chef's Table: Mountain Flavors from Asheville's Most Celebrated Chefs.*

Burgermeister's Feta-Sesame Burger

2 pounds ground beef
⅓ cup Worcestershire sauce
½ cup beer (use your favorite)

3 pieces feta cheese, crumbled
1 garlic clove, minced
½ teaspoon celery seeds
2 teaspoons cilantro
2 teaspoons toasted sesame oil
6 hearty buns
Leaf lettuce, tomato slices or any other assorted toppings of choice

Preheat the grill. Combine the ground beef, Worcestershire sauce and beer in a bowl and mix until combined. Mix the cheese, garlic, celery seeds, cilantro and sesame oil in a bowl, keeping the cheese chunky. Fold into the ground beef mixture. Divide into six equal portions. Shape each portion into a patty larger than the size of the bun to allow for shrinkage during grilling. Place on a grill rack and grill over medium-high heat for 4 minutes. Turn the patties and grill until cooked through. Place one patty on the bottom half of each bun. Top with leaf lettuce, tomato slices or any other toppings of choice. Top with the remaining half of the bun.

The staff of Burgermeister's loved to improvise, so when a snowstorm hit Asheville in 2010 someone from the restaurant went online to share this recipe on the Asheville snow blog.

Snow Cream

1 cup milk
2 tablespoons sugar
1 tablespoon vanilla

Stir ingredients until sugar dissolves and pour over 3 cups clean snow.

Source Materials

The bulk of research for this book took place at the North Carolina Room in Asheville's Pack Memorial Library, located downtown on Haywood Street. In addition to the databases accessible there the North Carolina Room houses hard copies of such reference works as city directories, indexed and bound newspaper files, menus and cookbooks.

Databases accessible there include the powerful search engine newspapers. com, which revealed not only news stories and promotional materials going back many years but also display advertisements, classified ads and crime citations; the North Carolina Room's own collections of digitized images, manuscripts, oral histories, maps and more, at ncroom.buncombecounty. org; and the full databases for the *Asheville Citizen-Times* and the *Mountain Xpress* newspapers.

Another important collection of historic materials, called Special Collections & University Archives, includes documents and outstanding photographic records of Asheville's past. These resources are housed at the University of North Carolina–Asheville, specifically, at the D.H. Ramsey Library. For online access, see toto.lib.unca.edu.

In order to confirm some background material, I did, in a few cases, refer back to my earlier book *Asheville: A History* (McFarland), because I trusted my own fact-checking.

Online restaurant reviews and blogs for lifelong Asheville residents show a darker side of the city's restaurant history. Traditional journalistic filters and balance are missing, so results can be more cutting, if still informative.

Recipe sources are credited individually.

There was no substitute for visiting the various restaurant sites, whether or not a restaurant still existed—the traffic, the sunlight, the skyline, the people walking about are all important in understanding the history of Asheville's lost restaurants and how they may have contributed to Asheville's restaurant scene today.

Index

About the Author

Award-winning investigative reporter Nan K. Chase has written for the *New York Times*, *Wall Street Journal*, *Washington Post* and *Miami Herald* and for magazines including *Air & Space*, *Atlanta Magazine* and *Blue Ridge Country*. She is the author of *Asheville: A History* and several other books. Nan is an avid gardener and shares her work @drinktheharvest.

Visit us at
www.historypress.com